Simple & Savvy Strategies For Creating Healthy Eaters

Beverly Pressey, M.S., R.D., Mom

simple & savvy

strategies for creating healthy eaters

GUILT FREE

Parent Tested!

Fortified with Humor!

Best for children 6 months to 6 years

Beverly Pressey, MS, RD, Mom

To order additional copies, please contact us.
Booksurge Publishing
www.booksurge.com
1-866-308-6235
orders@booksurge.com

Table of Contents

Introduction

Welcome to the world of parenting. For most of us it is an unknown world. Our parenting skills are an ongoing work-in-progress. Parenting gives the words "multi-tasking" and "time management" new meanings. We are now not only responsible for ourselves, but for another living being who we are just beginning to understand.

One of the challenges of parenting is realizing when you have done enough. Our newborns are so helpless that we do everything for them. But very quickly babies start to make sense of the world. My book provides you some guidelines for feeding so you know what to do and when you have completed your job. It is not your job to make a child or baby eat. It is not your job to offer different foods until a baby or child decides to eat something. It is not your job to provide five course dinners every night, unless you want to.

This book is for those who would like to raise a nutritionally and emotionally healthy child. Emotional health includes allowing a child to maintain his or her own innate ability to eat when they are hungry and stop when they are full. A nutritionally healthy child will intuitively choose the foods their body needs to grow and develop properly, as well as some fun food. Food choices will include a wide variety of foods and a willingness to try new foods. This is all possible, even if you have a busy life style.

There are many books on the market about children's nutrition and cookbooks. There are parenting books detailing lengthy true-to-life success stories of children benefitting when parents follow the author's plan. I, too, have a plan. It is simple and concise. My advice will save you time now and will save you time as your child gets older. It is easy to implement because it is based on common sense with a healthy dose of compulsive organizational suggestions thrown in. You will get practical and tactical information, not inspirational stories.

You deserve to know how to feed your child without becoming a chef, nutritionist, or child psychologist. This book covers what you need to know about nutrition, not everything there is to know about it. You will learn how to actually feed your child and what to expect from them. I will discuss the possible ways your child will try to undermine your efforts and how to prevail without arguments or punishments. You will also learn how to intelligently choose the foods that you want for your family and how to get meals on the table with the least amount of time and effort. Meal times can and should be enjoyable family time. Drop the guilt and enjoy eating with your child. Let me show you how easy it is, starting from the first bite your child takes.

Chapter 1

Feeding The First Year

First Foods

When to Start Solids

Feeding your baby brings up a multitude of issues. First you have
to decide to breastfeed or bottle feed your child. This decision will
see you through the first 4-7 months as all the nutrients your baby
needs are provided in formula or breast milk. Then you realize
that you that you will need to offer solid foods in addition to breast
milk or formula. This leads to a myriad of other issues and questions: when should I start solids? What foods should I offer? How
much should I feed? How often should I feed? How do I even
feed a baby?

Your child will let you know when he or she is ready to start solids.
Watch for the cues. My advice is to follow your child's lead, and
your common sense and intuition. There is no need to rush solid
food introduction. Don't start solids hoping to solve your child's
sleep problems. Although most mothers disagree, studies have
shown that eating solid foods does not help babies sleep through
the night. Starting foods earlier rather than later does not correlate
with entrance into Harvard.

Sometime between 4 and 8 months you will notice that your
child can sit up with minimal assistance, moves his head easily
and watches you intently as you eat. He may reach for your food
or make sounds while you eat. Your child is telling you that he
is ready to start solids. Physical development and eating abilities
advance together.

A child who has no ability to sit is not ready for solid foods. If you have a high chair that reclines, use it in this position only to keep your child at the table with you, not as a feeding position. Any age child fed in a reclining position is more likely to choke. For a baby just learning to control the food, it is a disaster. A child who can not turn his head from side to side can not communicate when he is done eating; this is essential for a healthy eating process.

Beginner Eaters

Age	4-8 months
Physical signs	Supported sitter Pushes up on arms (on tummy) with straight elbows Moves head forward to reach spoon Turns head away from spoon when full
Eating Methods	May push food out with tongue at first Moves food forward and back in mouth with tongue

Advanced Beginner Eaters

Age	5-9 months
Physical Signs	Sits independently Picks up and holds small objects Leans toward spoon or food
Eating Methods	Reaches for food Points toward food Slows eating when full Tightens lips or pushes food way when full Presses upper lip to draw food into mouth Rakes food toward self into fist Transfers food from one hand to other Drinks from parent held cup

Intermediate Eaters

Age	6-10 months
Physical Signs	Learns to crawl
	May pull up to stand
Eating Methods	Reaches and points to food when hungry
	Shows excitement for food when hungry
	Pushes food away when full
	Moves tongue side to side of mouth for mashing food
	Plays with spoon and brings to mouth, not self feeding
	Self feeding with fingers
	Holds cup independently
	Holds small food between thumb and index finger

How to Start Solids

What solid food should be fed first? Current research shows that texture is more important than food group, so start with semi-solids and thicken as time goes on. Many people start with rice cereal but soft banana, sweet potato mixed with breast milk or formula, and store-bought baby foods would be fine as well. The food should be the consistency of applesauce. Remember, we are offering solid food, not liquids on a spoon. There is no truth to the belief that feeding a baby fruits before vegetables will cause rejection of the vegetables because they are not as sweet at the fruit. You can introduce foods in whatever order you like, but the consistency of the food must be appropriate to avoid choking.

Iron stores start to decrease after 6 months, so foods with some iron are appropriate. In the United States we have iron fortified rice cereal. Rice cereal is the preferred delivery device for the iron, as rice is unlikely to cause an allergic reaction. Natural sources of iron include meats, poultry and fish, as well as beans, oatmeal, molasses and prunes. Never give a baby or child iron supplements unless prescribed by your doctor. An overdose of iron could be fatal.

To help you decide what foods to offer, refer to the following chart. The foods in this first column are appropriate for a new eater. The second column is foods for when your baby is ready for a little more texture. These babies can use their upper lip to draw food into their mouth and can transfer food from one hand to the other. Third are finger foods, for babies that are able to pick up very small objects with their index finger and thumb (this is called a pincer grasp) and can hold a cup independently. There are no store-bought baby foods on this list. Feel free to use them, but notice that you don't need to.

First Foods to 1st Birthday		
First Foods	**Second Foods**	**Third Foods**
Rice cereal	Refried beans (vegetarian)	Chex and Cheerios
		Mixed grain cereal
	Cheerio's-type cereal (Trader Joe's brand has no wheat, Cheerios has wheat bran)	Whole wheat noodles
Bananas, soft creamed with breast milk or formula		Quinoa, rice, millet, couscous, barley
		Canned salmon
	Oatmeal (cooked)	Soups, canned or homemade (pour off liquid & serve at room temp): chicken noodle, minestrone, beef barley, etc.
Avocado (pureed with water if needed)	Noodles (soft cooked): white wheat, rice, spelt, corn/quinoa	
		Meat loaf
		Frozen berries
Canned (pureed) pear, peach, mango, or apricot	Yogurt: soy or cow milk	Melon, watermelon, cantaloupe, honeydew (small pieces)
	Tofu	Soft skinless plums, peaches, pears and kiwi
Potato, yam, squash, sweet potato – baked and thinned with water	Cottage cheese	Grapes (seedless, cut into small pieces)
	Carrots or peas canned	Beans (canned): garbanzo, kidney, black, pinto, baked beans, etc.
	Broccoli florets (well cooked)	Pretzel and bread sticks
Carrots: soft steamed & pureed (fresh or frozen)		Toast
		Cheese (hard): colby, cheddar, jack (sticks or shredded)
		Veggie burgers
Applesauce: no sugar added	Steamed zucchini	Chili (canned or home-made)
		Macaroni and cheese
	Humus, bean dip	Lasagna, ravioli
		Fish sticks
Oat cereal	Polenta (corn grits)	Meats (soft, moist): beef, poultry, lamb, etc.
		Fish (deboned, flake): salmon, sole, halibut, etc.

To start feeding, put the baby in a sitting position, usually in a high chair or on your lap. Place a small amount of food on your finger tip or baby spoon. Offer it to the child, but do not put it into the baby's mouth. Let the child show you they are ready by opening their mouth or moving toward the spoon. Then place the food in their mouth and let them close their mouth over the food. Your child may, at first, push the food out with his or her tongue; this action is called "tongue thrust." If this is constant, the child may not be ready for solids. This tongue thrust action will quickly decrease when he is ready. Your child may also cough a few times (gagging) but the coughing will become infrequent or stop if the food is an appropriate texture.

Some babies insist on feeding themselves from the start. Let them. It's great for them to be able to explore their food and learn to find their mouth. Put the food on their tray and let them go at it. If this process seems too messy, put less food on your child's tray. You may also want to invest in the bibs with long sleeves or one with a catch pocket attached. You may also try feeding the baby with a spoon while they try to feed themselves. If your child constantly reaches for the spoon, give them their own. You can keep feeding with your spoon as they learn to use their own. Children learn to use a spoon between one and three years of age.

Gagging and Choking

Gagging is scary for the person feeding the baby, but it is a natural process as the baby gets used to swallowing. However, if gagging continues for more than a few coughs, the food offered is probably too thick or large. Choking is different than gagging and is a serious concern for the child. A choking baby is silent as the esophagus is blocked by the food. A choking baby will look like he is trying to cough something up but no food or sound is coming out. Sometimes the infant manages to push out the blocking food item, but don't wait for this to happen for more than a few seconds. Get help immediately. This can be serious and you should call 911 and administer basic infant first aid. Although any food can cause choking for any given child, choking can almost always be avoided. Ensure that the child is fed appropriate foods and texture, is sitting up, is not distracted by the television, toys, pets or books, and is supervised by an observant adult.

The following chart can help you decide what foods maybe inappropriate because of possible choking. In general, foods which have a thick consistency or are sticky, slippery, hard to chew, small or round are more likely to cause choking. Do keep in mind, though, that any food can cause a baby, child or adult to choke, so always supervise your child while they are eating.

Ages 1 -2 Years
Possible Choking Foods

Food of Concern	Tips
Crisp fruit such as apples and pears	Peel fruit, grate, slice thinly or steam
Raw carrots, peas and other vegetables	Steam, no raw vegetables until 2 year molars are in (back teeth)
Fiber-filled vegetables such as celery and fresh green beans	Cut into small pieces and steam or simmer until soft
Cherries with pits	Remove pits, cut cherries into smaller pieces
Grapes	Cut into smaller pieces, remove seeds
Hot dogs, sausages	Cut length-wise and then into smaller pieces
Meats	Moist meats are best, cut into small pieces, or shredded
Lettuce, spinach	Avoid raw leafy greens. Cut into small pieces and steam
Popcorn, tortilla chips	Avoid
Hard candy, chewing gum	Avoid
Nuts	Avoid until age 2 due to allergies, ground
Beans	Well cooked to soft, or mash
Noodles	Well cooked to soft
Cookies, teething biscuits	Soft cookies, avoid hard teething biscuits
Processed cheese	Avoid, too thick; use real grated cheese or small pieces of cheese
Peanut butter	Avoid until age 2 due to allergies; thin with water, applesauce or jelly, use thin layer on cracker or bread

Ages 3-6 Years Possible Choking Foods	
Food of Concern	**Tips**
Cherries with pits Grapes	Remove pits, cut into smaller pieces Cut into smaller pieces
Nuts	Grind or chop
Hot dogs, sausages	Cut length-wise and then into smaller pieces
Hard candy, chewing gum	Avoid
Popcorn	For good chewers only
Peanut butter	Thin with water, applesauce or jelly, use thin layer on cracker or bread
Crisp fruit such as apples and pears	Slice thinly
Raw carrots	Cut in sticks rather than rounds (coins)

Inappropriate Foods for Babies

In addition to choking foods, honey, including honey baked into crackers or cookies should be avoided. A botulism found in honey would cause a mature digestive system no or very little problems; however, it could be fatal to the immature digestive system of a child under the age of one. Some experts recommend not giving citrus (oranges, grapefruit, lemons, limes) to babies under age one or two because the high acid load may give a child severe diaper rash and possible diarrhea.

Parents often wonder about giving spicy or highly seasoned foods to infants. As the seasoning in other cultures may seem hot, spicy or strong to us, they are appropriate to that culture and given to their babies as part of the food introduction process. Also, if the mother is breastfeeding and eating spicy foods, the child is already receiving a watered-down version of these flavors. There are a few studies that show that breastfed babies are more open to new flavors and foods because breast milk has slightly different flavors depending on the diet of the mother whereas formula tastes the same every time.

Allowing your baby to try foods with spices is not a problem. You may actually find that a baby under the age of two is more open to

18

new flavors than a three or four year-old. Introducing these flavors early on however does not always result in the child having a continuous life-long acceptance. Many times a food a child readily accepted at 18 months is routinely rejected at a later age.

There is still research and controversy about fluoride in our drinking water and how much fluoride children need. As of 2007, the American Dentistry Association (ADA) recommended that babies fed formula (condensed or powdered) mixed with water should not use fluoridated water for this purpose. There is some concern that a baby exclusively fed formula mixed with fluoridated water may be at risk for problems with the development of tooth enamel. Bottled water that has been labeled purified, demineralized, deionized, distilled or reverse osmosis filtered water is fluoride free and can be used with formula. Occasional use of fluoridated water should not cause an increase in risk.

Until one year of age, instead of brushing a baby's teeth, use a soft wet cloth to wipe off your babies teeth before sleeping. It is advised by the ADA that you not use fluoride toothpaste before age two. Around age two, you can start with a small toothbrush and a very, pea-sized amount of tooth paste. As spit muscles may not be developed, check with your pediatrician about using fluoride or fluoride-free tooth paste. Monitor tooth brushing until age six, or until your child is able to spit well and avoid swallowing tooth paste. If you have any questions about tooth brushing and fluoride contact your pediatrician or dentist.

There is now some concern about the use of certain plastics in baby bottle nipples, baby bottles and the lining of cans of formula, both liquid and powdered. Concern about latex allergies from bottle nipples can be addressed by purchasing only silicone nipples. A common plastic called bisphenol A (BPA) has been found to be toxic when ingestion exceeds "safe" levels. Studies are revealing that some baby formula cans lined with BPA and baby bottles made with BPA may be leaching BPS in unsafe levels. To learn more about this topic, go to www.ewg.org/node/25637, a web site provided by the nonprofit organization Environmental Working Group (EWG). Their information is accurate and thorough. They recommend using glass bottles or those that do not have a number 7 or the letter PC stamped into the plastic of the bottle. In addition to providing information, EWG also list results of independent testing on the leaching of BPA from different canned formulas.

Increasing Solids

At first your child will eat very little; most of their nourishment comes from formula or breast milk. When your child begins to regularly eat approximately two tablespoons of food at a sitting, increase to two meals per day. In this way you can slowly increase meals until you are feeding solids four to six times a day. (Get use to it, you will be feeding them this often until they leave your house!) Try not to be too timid about increasing the solidity of foods offered. Remember, by one year most children are easily eating most table foods. An infant is most open to new foods, tastes and textures from four to twelve months. It is important to offer a variety of foods during this window of opportunity. If you are hesitant to try a new food or texture, do it when someone else is around. Bring the new food to a parent group, when visiting friends or when there is another adult at home with you.

As you increase the number of solid food meals, you may notice that your child's milk consumption is slowly decreasing. This is normal: as the child learns to eat more and a greater variety of foods, the need for breast milk or formula decreases. Continue to offer breast milk or formula with and/or between meals as needed. An infant just learning to try solids should probably be given breast milk or formula first so they are calm during the new experience of food. When your child acclimates to managing solids, around nine months of age, you may want to offer breast milk or formula after the solids. A child may be open to new tastes if they are a little bit hungry. You do not have to offer breast milk or formula at every feeding, or solids every time you offer breast milk or formula.

Do not withhold solids from a baby because they have no teeth. On average a baby will start showing teeth around six months. Some babies show their first teeth as early as four months and others as late as thirteen months. This is all normal. Whether they have teeth or not babies chew their food with their gums. Front teeth are for biting and ripping smaller pieces of food from larger pieces. Molars are the chewing teeth and they do not appear until a child's second year. An eleven-month-old child with no teeth can eat noodles as well as one with four teeth on top and bottom. They bring the food into their mouth, move it to their gums with their tongue, and chew way happily.

How Often to Feed a Baby

During the first year we feed our babies on demand, usually every 1½ - 2 ½ hours. Even if it appears that your child is not asking for food, offer it a least every 3 hours. Even when you're feeding them solids, continue to feed on demand during the first year, interspersing solids with breast milk or formula.

How often should a baby be fed solids? I always tell parents, "If it is your first child, feed them when you are bored. When it is your second (or third or fourth), whenever you have time." What I am trying to get across is that you don't need to feed solids the same time every day. Once you start one feeding of solids per day, continue until your baby shows readiness for a second feeding. Keep adding additional solid feedings until you have reached 4-6 solid food feedings a day. If a child is under age 1, still feed solids, formula or breast milk on demand. If you have a schedule that works for you and you baby, go for it. If you are not a schedule-person, your baby will be fine as long as you feed often enough.

When feeding solids, choose one or two foods and let your child eat until they show you that they are finished. They don't need more choices. If they don't eat either of the foods, the meal is over. Don't go to the fridge and get something else or cajole your child into eating. Babies eat when they are hungry and stop when they are full. Follow your child's lead and your own loving instincts.

How Much to Feed

How much should you feed your baby? As much as they want to eat. Don't expect your child to eat the same amount of food each day. One day they may eat one-quarter cup of applesauce and one-half of a banana at lunch. The next day they won't touch a banana and will eat only one tablespoon of food at lunch time. This is normal. Their hunger will differ from day to day and week to week. Our children know when they need to eat. Our job is to consistently offer appropriate foods on a regular basis.

The amount of food a child eats is determined by his or her internal cues. They will sense a growth spurt and eat more, or an illness and eat less. They take their cues from their developmental and health needs.

Our children, at infancy, eat when they are hungry and stop when they are full. They do not eat from boredom, excitement, fear, loneliness, happiness or sadness. They do not monitor their eating based on photographs from fashion magazines or movie stars or in order to fit into last year's dress. We need to let children learn to trust their instincts. We do this by trusting the child to eat as much or as little as they want. We want our children to eat because they are hungry and stop when they are full (or sated). A child that responds to this internal cue will have a life free of eating to satisfy other needs.

Do you have one of those charts listing how much of what food a child of each age should eat per day? Get rid of it. Every child develops differently; therefore, a chart dictating exact foods and amounts should be used only as a guide. Even if you offer the exact foods listed on a chart your child will not eat the prescribed amount. If you insist on them eating the prescribed amount you may end up feeling like a "bad mother" when they don't eat what you have been told they should eat, or you may worry about your child's nutrition and growth.

Worse, you may over feed a child who is not hungry or underfeed a child who is very hungry. You cannot over feed a baby unless you are constantly and consistently feeding her when she's shown you that she's finished eating. There are many signals babies use to tell us they are done eating. They may turn their head away from the food, tighten their lips, arch their back and head away from the food, start playing or throwing food. Forcing a baby to continue eating after these signals may teach him not to trust his own internal signals. Telling a baby to eat more because "Mommy loves a big boy," "Daddy is so proud of you when you eat all of your food," "one more bite for Grandma," and etc, will teach your child to eat to receive your approval and love. Now eating becomes associated with emotions. Babies will overeat to retain your love and acceptance. The goal for babies and children is for them to eat when they are hungry.

22

Food Rejection

As your children approach their first birthdays, offer a variety of foods during the day and allow your child to choose from the foods you offer. Sometime during the day offer fruits, vegetables, carbohydrates, fats and protein. Don't worry if your child doesn't eat a certain food; research has shown that children sometimes need to see food eight to ten times before trying it. Most parents will stop offering a food after it has been rejected three or four times.

The best way to encourage a child to try a new food is for them to see it regularly. When parents model eating these foods, children are more apt to eat them. You don't need to say anything to the child about trying the food but you could say, "This broccoli is really crunchy." Don't forget- once you have offered foods, your job is done. Allow your child to eat or not. A child offered a variety of healthy foods four to six times a day will not allow themselves to be hungry or have a nutritional deficiency. They will eat to meet their needs.

My son tested us on this theory. My husband pointed out that my son only ate when he really liked the food. He would not eat the healthier foods and would wait until the fun foods were available to him. As I observed my son I saw that my husband was correct, but only until a certain point. After a few days of living on chocolate milk, cookies, and rice or bread he would start to voluntarily eat healthier foods. All of a sudden he would eat a few apple slices, some refried beans and cheese. Eventually his body told his brain it was time to eat something nutritious, and without a degree in nutrition he picked the right foods, because they were available to him.

Allergies

In order to detect any allergies, start with one food and wait three to four days. If there are no observable changes in your child, add another new food to your infant's diet. You may repeat the first food again during this time. If no unusual reaction occurs after this time, offer another new food, and wait another three to four days. If a reaction occurs, the newest food is the possible allergen. Continue to add foods one every three to four days, including previously offered foods, until you have tried all foods. This actually goes more quickly than you may think.

Invite a few families to a party and you may end up with a list of food allergies. Allergies do seem to be on the rise and many parents worry about possible food allergies developing in their babies. Documented peanut allergies doubled from 1997-2001. However, keep in mind that only 5% of children and only 2% of adults have actual allergies. So that leaves approximately 3% of adults that had allergies as children but have out grown them. Many allergies discovered before age three will disappear in as little as three months. Studies have shown that 85% of allergies to egg, milk and soy are outgrown by age five and even one out five peanut allergies are resolved by age five as well. Tree nut and seafood allergies are rarely outgrown.

Studies of allergies within families show that if both parents or one child and one parent have a food allergy, subsequent children have a 70-80% change of having a food allergy. If only one parent has a food allergy this number drops to 40-50%. If one child has a food allergy, the chance of a subsequent child having a food allergy is 7%. If you have any history of food allergy in your family it is best to consult your pediatrician or allergist before starting food introduction. Otherwise, milk products eggs, soy, wheat, and fish can be introduced before one year of age.

Signs and Symptoms

Any food is a potential allergen. Over 90% of food allergies come from eight foods: milk, egg, tree nuts, soy, wheat, shell fish, peanuts and fish, however all foods should be introduced one at a time. Food should be introduced two separate times before it can be determined that there is no allergy. After each introduction look for any unusual signs or symptoms such as diarrhea, cramps, hives, eczema, itching, vomiting, swelling or swelling of the lips or tongue. Signs of an allergy usually occur quickly – either immediately or within 2 hours of eating the food. All breathing problems or swelling that causes breathing problems should be acted on immediately. Call 911. The operator can assist you until professional help arrives. Other symptoms should be reported immediately to your pediatrician or allergist so you can take proper action and receive information on allergy diagnosis and treatment.

Sometimes, however, symptoms may develop hours or even days after the new food was introduced. Is this an allergy or is it something else? Maybe it is a cold, teething, or a rash from new clothes or soap? It's not always totally obvious that a food caused an unusual symptom. If you think it is the food and the symptom was not life-threatening, write down what you fed your child, how much you fed the child, how soon after the food was eaten that the symptom occurred and what the symptom was. Report this to your pediatrician or allergist before you try this food again. Sometimes the second introduction of a food can trigger a more severe reaction.

Food Intolerance

Sometimes our children have reactions to foods that are not caused by an allergy, but by intolerance to a food. What is the difference? An allergic reaction is an immune response. The body senses a particular food as foreign and hostile to the body. The immune system sends out defensive cells to attack; these defensive cells also cause the symptoms that we observe. Intolerance is not an immune response, but is still a bodily reaction to the food.

The most common example of food intolerance is lactose intolerance. Those with lactose intolerance do not produce the naturally occurring enzyme called lactase that aids in the breaking down of the sugar molecules in milk, called lactose. When this sugar is not broken down during digestion, the large sugar molecules can cause abdominal cramping as they move through the small intestines. As sugar molecules attract water molecules, the large intestine is over loaded with water; therefore diarrhea is also a symptom of lactose intolerance. There are other types of intolerances such as headaches caused by chocolate or asthma triggered by sulfites. Avoidance of the food is the best way to handle food intolerances.

Can Allergies Be Prevented?

Recent research shows that the mother's diet during pregnancy and during lactation (breastfeeding) do not have "significant roles" in the prevention of allergies and asthma. The mother's diet during lactation my have some protection for eczema. For children at high risk for allergies, (either parent has at least one allergy) exclusive breastfeeding for four months was found to be protective for milk and other allergies for up to two years of age. It was also found that soy-based formulas did not seem to prevent allergies. For more guidance, consult with a nutritionist or health care provider to guide you during food introduction.

To decrease the likelihood of allergies it has been common practice to wait for an infant to become a certain age before introducing certain foods into a baby's diet. As peanut allergies have doubled in the last 5 years, doctors recommended the delay of their introduction until the child is two years-old in hopes of decreasing this trend. This is now being questioned by Allergists and Pediatricians as recent research puts past policies into question. The American Academy of Pediatrics revised it's policy statement regarding food introduction in January 2008. Where it previously did not recommended introduction of liquid cow's milk, egg white and peanuts until after age one or longer, their current policy states that they no longer find "convincing evidence" to delay these foods until after age one. However they continue to recommend waiting until age four to six month before introducing any solid foods.

What could waiting a few months accomplish? Wouldn't a child with an allergy have an allergy no matter when a food is introduced? Can an allergy be caused by introducing a food too soon? The answers are both yes and no. Some babies will develop allergies no matter how conscientious you are about food introduction and timing. But some allergies might be avoided or symptoms of allergies lessened by not introducing foods until a baby shows signs of readiness for foods and waiting to introduce some specific foods. Remember, it is still not recommended to introduce any solids before four to six months of age.

Why might delaying work? One theory goes like this: think of your child's digestive system as a tube going down the center of the body. This tube has openings at the mouth and at the anus. When a baby is born this tube is not fully mature and the baby's immune system is not fully developed. In a newborn baby, this tube has microscopic holes in it that become even smaller as the baby becomes older. If a baby is given a food, and during digestion microscopic bits of the food leave this tube through the holes, the baby's immune system sees these bits as foreign invaders. The body sends in cells to destroy or contain them. These destroyer cells are called antibodies. Once the body develops antibodies, it creates a ready army of these food specific antibodies ready and waiting to be discharged every time the body senses this same foreign food anywhere in the body.

There may or may not be any obvious reaction to a discharge of antibodies the first time the body senses the foreign invader. However, the second time this foreign invader is encountered by the body, not just in the digestive systems but perhaps in the skin, tongue or even the nose, it will mount a massive attack of antibodies. This attack is known to us as an allergic reaction and may be as mild as a slight rash or as serious as anaphylactic shock, a life-threatening situation wherein the body goes into shock and immediate medical attention is needed.

However, as a baby grows and matures, the digestive system matures as well. This tube becomes semi-permeable: properly allowing vitamins, minerals and sugars to move into the blood stream from the tube, but making sure that improperly digested materials do not leak out. Therefore waiting until the digestive system is mature may possibly avoid an allergy or lessen the severity of allergy symptoms.

There is also the hygiene theory of allergy prevention. It theorizes that due to the clean environment many of us live in, where disinfectants, hand washing and vaccines are part of a healthy life style, the part of the immune system developed to fight parasites doesn't have enough to do so it starts attacking proteins in food and air

Living with Food Allergies

If you suspect a food allergy, contact your health care provider. Once a food allergy has been diagnosed by your health care provider or other specialist, you will need continued help to monitor it and identify which foods and ingredients to avoid. Contact a nutritionist for help with food selection and to be sure your child's nutritional needs are met while avoiding certain foods. Contact the American Dietetic Association's website www.eatright.org to find a registered dietitian in your area. The Food Allergy & Anaphylaxis Network (www.foodallergy.org) is a non-profit organization that can help you with find a local support group, research, resources, recipes and advocacy information. The information can be especially helpful as your child starts school and you are concerned about safe guarding his diet away from home. Understanding and Managing your Child's Food Allergies by Scott H. Sicherer, M.D., clearly explains the complexity of allergy diagnosis and how to deal with allergies from a food and emotional perspective.

Whether your child has allergies or not, if he's enrolled in child care many of you will be asked to pack a peanut-free lunch. This should not be too difficult with the following chart of peanut butter sandwich alternatives. Also, keep in mind that even by omitting a peanut butter sandwich from a lunch, your child will receive protein from milk and milk products, grains and vegetables. Furthermore, you can give your child protein in their breakfast before they leave home, or provide them with a protein food at a home snack and/or dinner.

Alternatives to Peanut Butter and Tree Nuts

Ideas for Children's Meals and Snacks
When Nut Products Need to be Avoided

Children who have allergies to nuts may have life threatening reactions to extremely small quantities of any nut product.

Protein Lunch Ideas

✓ Tahini (sesame butter)-use as a dip for soft veggies or as a spread

✓ Tuna, salmon (canned) with mayonnaise or dry

✓ Cooked chicken or turkey: sandwiches, drumsticks, thighs, etc.

✓ Deli meats

✓ Eggs- egg salad or hard boiled

✓ Cold cooked salmon

- ✓ Yogurt
- ✓ Cold rice salad with peas and corn
- ✓ Cheese (cubes, string cheese, grated, spreads, cold pizza or grilled cheese sandwiches)
- ✓ Cold Pasta Salad with cheese, beans, or chicken
- ✓ Beans (refried in a tortilla, bean salad, bean dip, humus)
- ✓ Cottage Cheese (with fruit)
- ✓ These foods are peanut, free but some individuals with peanut allergies also need to avoid legumes, soy beans, tree nuts or other foods.
- ✓ Soy Butter (use it just like peanut butter)
- ✓ Tofu, Tempeh

Caution

Avoid cross contamination. Wash and sanitize all cutting surfaces and knives after handling peanut butter. Wash hands thoroughly. Residual peanut butter on surfaces can transfer to "peanut free" foods and cause an allergic reaction.

Almost all sports and breakfast bars contain nuts or are processed in a facility that processes nut products.

Weaning From Breast or Bottle to Cup

When to Wean a Breast Fed Baby

Weaning from the breast or bottle can range from an easy and natural transition to a difficult emotional challenge for both you and your baby. Some children will naturally wean from the breast, rejecting it in favor of a cup or bottle. Bottle feeders may have no problem switching to a cup. All babies can make the change with your support.

As breastfeeding may continue as long as the mother and child desire, when to wean is a personal decision. Try to let the decision be yours, although you will find that friends, family and even strangers let you know their opinions. If you want to continue breastfeeding and your child is showing less interest, The La Leche League is an organization that provides information and support for nursing mothers and their families. You can use their website for information and to find local and personal support. (www. lalecheleague.org) If you experience trouble with breastfeeding you can also receive support from your pediatrician or a lactation specialist. However, if you are ready or you are okay about your baby being ready, it's time to wean.

How to Wean From Breast or Bottle to Cup

There are many different ways to go about weaning from the breast or bottle but overall it is a game of distraction and change of habit. Do you feed your child in the same room, in the same chair, with the same music, holding the child in a specific way? These are all places to make changes to create a new routine for your child. Make sure you are in a different room or sitting in a non-feeding place when you think your baby may be ready to feed. Don't hold your child in the feeding position, this may remind him of breast or bottle feeding.

You can create a distraction by involving in play activity during the usual feeding time or by having a meal of solid food and either milk or water in a cup. If you are the one who regularly feeds your child, try having another adult available to feed using a cup instead of a bottle. For this to be particularly effective and less stressful for you, plan to be away from the house at this time.

Over the course of the day a child has probably developed a bottle or breast feeding time that is more important, either nutritionally or emotionally. This is the last bottle or breast feeding that you want to eliminate. Start with an easier one, maybe mid-morning or afternoon. These are great times for snacks. You can wean slowly, changing one feeding time or style a week, or faster, making a change every couple of days. Weaning slowly will likely be less stressful for your child and you. There are definitely times not to try weaning your baby. If there is a major change occurring for you, your baby or in the household, it is not a good time to introduce another change.

Times not to Wean

- ✓ Traveling or spouse traveling

- ✓ Guest living in your house

- ✓ Illness

- ✓ Remodeling in your home

- ✓ New job for you, including a change of work schedule

- ✓ New nanny or child care situation

- ✓ Frantic holiday season

- ✓ Immediately after the birth of a new child or introducing an adopted child into the family

Of course, given how busy our lives are, it may be impossible to avoid all of these times and still wean a child. Start when you think is best. If you have to stop at a certain point because of unexpected change, just stay where you are, in a holding pattern, until you can move on again. If you are weaning from the breast you can intentionally stop at a certain number or times of feedings. For example, you might want to wean a breastfed baby from daily nursing so you can return to work or have more freedom during the day, but continue evening or morning nursing, or both. Your breast milk production will adjust to meet your new feeding frequency or schedule. You can continue with limited nursing as long as you would like. You can usually avoid engorgement of your breasts or any associated discomfort with a slow weaning schedule. If you do have difficulties with engorgement or infection call your Ob/gyn, lactation consultant or check with near by hospitals for lactation information.

Before one year of age, any milk offered should be formula or expressed breast milk. After age one, cow's milk is appropriate if your child has no dairy allergies. During weaning you can offer the appropriate milk with or without food. At meals, to encourage drinking from the cup, offer milk before the food when the child is most hungry. You do not have to offer milk with every meal or snack. Remember, your child only needs a maximum of sixteen ounces of milk a day at age one.

Cup Drinking

Whether your child is breast or bottle fed, the time you spend feeding them is one of bonding and love, so weaning to a cup is more about emotion than nutrition. A child may resist breaking the habit of bottle and breastfeeding because they don't want to lose you. During this time make sure that you and other important adults are spending close, quiet time with your child. Let them know that they can have you even if they are not being fed.

Bottle feeding should be replaced with cup feedings around one year of age. Breastfeeding can continue as long as desired by the parent. However, even breastfed babies should be taught to use a cup around one year of age. All babies can be prepared for this transition by offering water in a cup or sippy cup around seven months of age. At seven months some babies are able to understand the sucking and swallowing motions to use a cup. Before age one, drinking from a cup is for practice; babies won't get much from the cup so don't use it for formula. Juice in a cup is also not recommended. Although the sweet taste of juice acts as an incentive, this can have consequences when a child will drink only juice from a cup. When at a table and eating with your child, an open cup or cup with a straw should be used, not a sippy cup. The way a child drinks from these cups is quite different. The use of bottles, pacifiers and sippy cups is facilitated by a flat tongue under the nipple or spout. The use of an open cup allows the child to use different muscles, those that are important to speech. A child actually uses more muscles to use a sippy cup than an open cup. Also, paper cups are not recommended. A child needs to feel a firm cup in her hands and against her lip. A paper cup will give way and not allow proper muscle usage. However, when spilling is an issue, perhaps in the car or when a child is not closely supervised, or when you are in a hurry, a sippy cup may be more convenient and practical.

Transition to Cow's Milk

In addition to transitioning to a cup at one year of age, this is also the time to move from formula to milk. Your child can eliminate formula from their diet at one year of age because they should now be eating a wide variety of foods in ample quantity to meet many of their nutritional needs. Formula and breast milk are complete foods; milk is not. Milk is a good source of calcium, vitamin D, protein and fat. All other minerals, vitamins, and other kinds of fats and carbohydrates need to be provided via solid food. By one year, your child has evolved from getting his nutrition from what he eats rather than what he drinks. If your child is still breastfed at age one, you do not need to introduce cow's milk; you can add cow's milk to your child's diet but it is not necessary as all of the nutrients (and more) of cow's milk are provided by the breast milk.

Some parents tell me that they continue to use formula after age one to make sure their baby is getting all the nutrients that they need. Although well-meaning, this approach can inhibit a baby from accepting a variety of solid foods. If the caloric and nutritional needs of a baby arc met by the formula they have no internal queues to try solids. Formula was good when your child was unable to chew and swallow solids; it is a crutch for a child able to chew and swallow.

At one year of age a baby needs only a maximum of sixteen ounces of milk as they are incorporating the nutrients of a variety of solid foods into their diet. If they are allowed more milk, they will not be hungry for solid foods that provide nutrients that the milk doesn't contain. So you usually don't have to worry about your child getting enough milk even though she was previously consuming 28-34 ounces per day. If you are breastfeeding and have no way of knowing how much milk your child is receiving, don't worry. Your child will most likely start nursing less often or take in less milk at each feeding as their consumption of solids increases.

But will your child drink cow's milk? You have been introducing new foods to your baby for the past six to eight months, most of which they have accepted. So they will probably like milk as well. You don't need to offer milk combined in some amount with formula or breast milk as a transition. Just give them the milk. As this is a new food, they may accept it in the cup as they are not used to having it in a bottle. If your child does not appear to like milk do not despair. Remember, some children need to taste a new food eight to ten times before they decide it is ok. You may also want to serve the milk at room temperature, as your child's previous liquids and most foods were not served cold. I would use chocolate milk or other flavored milks as a last resort. The nutrition is the same but the sugar content is higher. Remember, my son does in fact drink chocolate milk. My daughter drinks no milk at all. If after several weeks your child will not drink milk, the nutritional components can be met with solid foods such as dairy products, greens and beans. Two to three servings of a dairy food will provide needed calcium. If you are concerned, speak to your health care provider.

The American Academy of Pediatrics (AAP) recommends whole milk from age one to two because of the fat content: 49%. Low fat milk (2% milk) is actually 34% calories from fat. We want our babies to have about 40% of calories from a variety of fats in their diets. The fat in whole milk is a saturated fat, the type considered unhealthy. So, using low fat milk would be acceptable as long as you are making sure there are other sources of fat in your babies' diet. Also, if you are buying milk for other family members, it may be more practical to buy the same kind of milk for all: 2% is a good choice without compromising nutrition. For more information on milk, refer to the chapter "Milk and All it's Various Forms".

Chapter 2

AGE ONE AND BEYOND

You Can Lead a Child to Food But You Can't Make Him Eat

Growth Slows

The nutritional needs of toddlers are different from children under age one. Growth rate slows after two years and calories needed per pound of body weight decrease. It may seem like your two year-old is eating less than at 18 months, and she likely is. As a one year-old triples his weight in the first year, between ages two to three years a child may gain only 4-6 pounds. The rapid physical and mental changes of the first two years are over. Overall development is slowing down.

However, brain growth continues at a rapid rate. By the end of a child's second year the brain has reached 75% of its adult size. Therefore, include healthy fats (vegetable fats) and limit saturated or partially hydrogenated fats and fried foods. Continue to offer whole grains, fruits, vegetables and proteins.

By age two and a half, most children have all 20 baby teeth. It is now time to start to incorporate some of the fresh fruits and vegetables that were choking hazards before your child had molars (the back chewing teeth). To avoid choking, start with small pieces of harder foods. Avoid fibrous vegetables such as celery and raw green beans. Fruits may need to be peeled. Ensure that the food is either cut up in small pieces or is large enough for a child to pick up and take a bite with their teeth. For safety, children should eat sitting down. Always monitor your child for any problems.

Food Phobias + Independence = Parenting Challenges

A toddler's appetite is often erratic. Your child may eat vastly different quantities and types of foods day to day or week to week. This is normal; follow the child's lead. Offer them nutritious foods. Let them eat as much of the offered foods as they want when hungry and let them stop when they are full, no matter how little or how much they eat. Keep in mind that their stomachs are small- only about the size of their fist- so they cannot be expected to eat large amounts at any one sitting. Toddlers are known to reject foods that they previously enjoyed. Despite the number of times you point this out to them, it makes no difference. They are now more aware of their environment and realize that there could be danger about. Acceptance of foods starts with frequent exposure to the food. So, continue to offer the foods you would like them to eat.

Toddlers are also starting to assert their independence and power. They have learned the power of "no" and may say it for the thrill rather than for the meaning. As a parent I have made the mistake of asking, "Do you want some apple?" But I quickly recovered by serving the apple anyway. Surprisingly, or maybe not, the apple was eaten. This is one reason to not ask our children what they want. If they say "no," it's over or there is an argument. Simple serve your child the apple.

Very quickly your toddler or preschooler will develop food preferences. We know what foods we would like our children to eat, so how do we get them to eat them? Do they really reject certain foods just because they know it's important to us that they eat them? Perhaps young children just don't like the color green. Is texture or smell a problem for some children? Are picky eaters made or born? Research is showing there is a genetic link, but in my experience, it is a little of everything. Due to your temperament or theirs, some children are more apt to try new foods or enjoy a wide range of food tastes, textures, looks and smells. Other children do not appear to be open to variety, and some fall in between these two extremes.

Researchers are finding that breastfed babies are more likely to accept a variety of tastes as they were exposed to slight variations of taste in breast milk, depending on the diet of the mothers. Whether your child is breast or formula fed, they should be given a wide variety of tastes, textures and smells when you are introducing different solid foods. Between four months and one year children are developmentally open to new foods and their associated characteristics.

Part of food acceptance is the smell and texture of food. Allow your child to explore the food, especially as a baby. Let them touch it, smear it, smell it. This is all part of the process for them. Their sense of smell is more intense than ours. They have more taste buds than adults and taste buds on the outside of their mouths, which disappear with age.

Acceptance of a new food is sometimes immediate and long-lasting. Others times a food is accepted the first time but rejected the next. Some children need to see a food 8-10 times before they decide to eat it. You may see a baby try a new food and make a face that we interpret as not liking the food. But if you continue to feed that food, the baby continues to open his mouth for the food. All of these behaviors are normal and children can display all of them at any given meal or day.

Timing

Beyond the taste, appearance, texture and smell of meals and snacks, timing is crucial in helping your child to try new foods. Try not to feed a child an hour and a half before the next meal or snack. We want children to come to meals a little hungry; this encourages them to try new foods. For the first year we feed an infant on demand. After that we slowly move toward scheduled meals and snacks. Scheduled meals and snacks do not mean that you feed your child at the exact same time each day as most of our lives don't work like that. It means that we offer our children food on a regular basis, before they are over the edge with hunger.

For most of our children this means offering food every 1½ hour to 3 hours. Even if a child does not ask to be fed, never let more than 3 hours go by without offering food. This teaches our children to go without food for small periods of time and helps them to understand the feeling of hunger. This also teaches our children to trust us in meeting their feeding needs on a regular basis.

A child who is not fed regularly will compensate. A child who is fed too often they can be very particular about what they choose to eat, as they are really not too hungry. They choose only to eat their favorite. There is no motivation to try something new and healthy. More seriously, a child not fed often enough will overeat because they are worried that they will become uncomfortably hungry before there are next fed. If your child regularly seems to eat excessive amounts of food at a sitting it may be that they are not fed often enough or on a regular basis. They do not trust that their food needs will be met so they stock up when they are fed.

But this does not guarantee an adventurous eater. My son, dutifully breastfed for 13 months and introduced to a wide variety of food by a trained professional (me), is not willing to try most new foods. But remember, research tells us that children may need to see a food 8-10 times before they are willing to try it. So I keep offering and after months of seeing a certain recipe he has occasionally asked for a taste, and liked it. The most crucial window for introducing variety is the first 6 months of food introduction. Don't wait. A child not given the opportunity to try different tastes and textures during this time will have a harder time adjusting to the food in general.

What to Do and Not to Do

Let's say that your child, like my son, is cautious of the food she tries. You know what you would like your child to eat. How do you get her to eat it? The first rule is: You decide what to offer and when. You have done your job and should receive the gold star of parenting if you offer your child a variety of healthy food four to six times over the course of the day. Six times is really not that many: breakfast, snack, lunch, snack, dinner, and maybe another snack.

The second rule is: your child decides whether to eat it or not, how much to eat and what order to eat offered foods. If you offer your child saltines, cheese and carrots, they get to eat the crackers first if they want to. They get to eat as many crackers as are available. If they only eat the crackers, this is fine. If you don't want your child to eat too many crackers because they are fun foods (foods that don't help you grow big and strong but are fun to eat) only provide what you think is an appropriate amount. Tell your child that there will be five crackers because they are just for fun. When the crackers are gone and your child asks for more remind them that crackers are a fun food but if they are hungry, there is still cheese and carrots. As these are healthy or growing foods, let them eat as much of these foods as they want. Don't feel obligated to offer more than two or three foods at any meal or snack. This is enough for a child; more choices would be distracting. Plus, three foods six times a day are more than enough of work for you.

Let your child eat as much as they want of the foods you offered, unless a fun food has a limit. This allows a child to be able to leave a meal or snack feeling sated, like they have had enough. This lets them develop a sense of trust in you (you let them stop eating when they say so) and a trust in themselves. Infants and children know when their body has had enough food if we let them stay in touch with this natural feeling. They will also learn that we trust them to make this decision for themselves. We do not encourage them to eat after they said or showed they are finished. We want children to grow up being fully engaged in their sense of hunger or satiety. This will keep them from disordered eating behaviors later in life.

So your child, who has only eaten the crackers, announces that he is finished. You have your doubts that he's eaten enough to last him until the next meal and you are not pleased that he did not eat any of the healthy foods. Remembering the second rule, you can simply say, "Don't forget, there will not be any food until after…" (Pick an activity they can relate to, not a time, such as after nap or after you watch TV or after Daddy gets home.) "If you are hungry you need to eat now." If they came to the snack hungry and they know they will really not get any food until the time you mentioned, they may choose to eat something else. If they ask for more crackers say "We're not having any more crackers because they are just for fun, but we have carrots or cheese if you are hungry." This may convince a child to eat a new or less favored food. If they still choose not to eat, the snack is over. Even if you don't think your child understands the words that you are saying, say them anyway. This lets you practice responding in this manner, and lets your child start hearing and making sense of the words.

For this to work, you must consistently follow through. If a child rejects all of the food you chose, do not jump up and get something else. They will never have reason to try a new food if you do this every time. They will learn that if they reject your choices they can have what they like. If you jump up and grab another food, you've provided your child with power and entertainment. If two or more adults at the table argue over whether or not to give the child another food, this is even better for the child: more power and even more entertainment.

If your child refuses to eat anything after you have reminded him that this is the time to eat, have him sit at the table as others eat, maybe five minutes for a two year-old and 15 minutes for a five year-old. Sometimes a hungry child sitting at a table with nothing to do will ask for some food, especially if they haven't eaten for a while. If they do, give it to them without comment. You can also tell a child who does not want to eat that meals are family time; if he doesn't want to eat it is okay, but he needs to spend time with the family. Make sure they know that even if they choose not to eat they will not be allowed to immediately go back to their previous activity. Many children will choose toys, television, computers or playing over food if given the choice.

As per rule two, a child should never be required to take a bite. Do allow a child to touch the foods or even put it in his mouth and spit it out (politely) if he doesn't like it. A child is more likely to try new foods if he knows he can retreat if he doesn't like the taste, texture or smell. The more foods a child tries, the more foods he will actually eat. Don't give up after three or four times. Keep serving what you want to eat and what you would like your child to enjoy. Seeing the family eat the foods is the best motivator.

After a meal or snack is finished, a child who refused to eat or ate very little may ask for some food. Do not respond to this plea with food. This teaches a child that if they can make it through a meal or snack, they can get what they want right after the meal or snack. You can respond with total sympathy and empathy; tell them that you would be hungry, too, if you just ate crackers for snack. Remind them that they chose not to eat and they now have to wait until the next scheduled eating time for food, even if that is the next morning.

Now this may sound harsh, especially for children between the ages of one and four. These children are just learning language and about action and consequences. For younger children (under three years of age), if they choose not to eat tell them there will be no food until the next snack, but don't wait three hours from the previous meal or snack. Use your judgment with the timing; let them be hungry for a little while without going over the top. Waiting 35 minutes may be enough for a one year-old. A four year-old may be able to wait up to one-and-a-half hours.

A normal child who eats four to six times a day will not suffer from any nutritional deficiencies if he chooses to skip a meal. Nor will he suffer from starvation. He will feel hungry and this is the consequence of choosing not to eat. The consequence is self–imposed; you offered them food and they chose not to eat. Many of us want our children to eat well for their health, but also ours. We don't want to be woken up at night by a hungry child. Don't worry. Most children will not wake up in the middle of the night hungry, and if they do, do not feed them. Food at night once develops into a pattern of wanting food at night. Acknowledge their hunger with as much or little sympathy as you like and remind them that they chose not to eat when food was offered. I suggest saying something like, "I would be hungry, too, if I chose not to eat dinner." If a child is thirsty, only provide water. Get through this one or two nights and you are home free. Feed the child and you are now providing food 24 hours a day. The bonus of a child hungry is that you have a motivated eater at breakfast and at other meals and snacks as they learn that they may feel hungry if they choose not to eat at snacks or meals.

Bribing, Rewarding, and Punishing

If a child eats nothing at a meal and five minutes later expresses hunger, should you give back the plate of food? No. The child needs to wait until the next snack. Should you bring the plate back at the next snack? This brings us to rule number three: never punish, reward or bribe with food. To bring back the same food is a punishment. The child has already rejected that food. Offer something else, but as always, you decide what to offer and when. Rewarding, bribing or punishing a child for eating or not eating teaches a child to eat for reasons other than hunger. This tells the child that you do not trust their sense of hunger or satiety. They learn that they should eat to please you, get something or avoid something unpleasant. This does not lead to healthy eating practices. Many studies are finding that the more we micromanage the way our children eat, the more likely they are to eat for the wrong reasons, which usually leads to over eating.

Bribing to eat food can also get out of hand. As your children realize how important it is to you that they eat certain foods, they use this to their advantage. They may not eat just to see you beg (entertainment and power) or they may not eat in order to get something from you: a toy or a fun food. As they get older they up the ante. Do you want to buy a Porsche for a teenager who eats three peas? Perhaps this is an exaggeration, but you get the idea. This rewarding and punishing becomes even more complicated if you have more than one child. Which child gets the reward, the one who ate two bites of chicken or the one who ate one bite of broccoli? Your children will also keep track better than you will. They will tell you with certainty, "Jamie got to eat dessert when he ate only one pea, why do I have to eat two?" Who wants to decide, who wants to keep track? You will be eating thousands of meals with your children. Many parents tell me that bribing works, but do you want to go through this every time you eat together? Or do you want your child to eat when they are hungry and stop when they are full?

So should a child who eats nothing at dinner receive dessert? Yes. If this child doesn't receive dessert he is being punished for not eating while the child who "eats enough" is rewarded. This is a clear violation of rules two and three. If you choose to offer dessert as part of the dinner meal, everyone should have access to it. What about children who will not eat dinner because they know they can fill up on dessert? If dessert is a healthy food, why do you care if they eat it instead of dinner? If dessert is a fun food, the child should be offered a child portion and told that as it is a fun food and when it is gone it is gone. Children may at first think this dessert without dinner deal is great; however, it usually back fires on them. A fun dessert will not satisfy a hungry child for long. Soon after consuming only dessert for dinner, this child will likely be hungry and ask for food. This is when you say empathetically, "I would be hungry, too, if I only ate dessert for dinner. Do you remember you chose not to eat dinner?" Do not feed this child until the next scheduled meal or snack. At the next snack or meal choose what to offer and serve it without comment. If the child never eats dinner and only eats the dessert this is fine, too. If he is offered food four to five other times a day and healthy foods are offered at these times, the child will have no nutritional problems. Maybe he is just not hungry at dinner time.

You can also serve the dessert as part of the dinner. Of course the child will eat the dessert first, but if this is a fun food they will only be allowed one serving. As they are sitting at the table watching others eat it may become clear to them that they are not satisfied yet, they need more to eat. Dinner is the only food available and your child will ask for it. Success! They are asking for food, you are not demanding that they eat it and you didn't even have to bribe them.

Some parents have told me that they can "get their child to eat" if they allow the child to play with a toy or watch TV. This is a classic example of winning a battle but losing the war. The parent may be pleased that the child is eating the "proper" foods in the "right" amounts, but what is the child learning? A child who eats without paying any attention to what he's eating is not in touch with his own needs. This child loses all sense of hunger or satiety. This is a child who is eating to please a parent or eating in order to be allowed to watch a movie. This is a child who is not learning to enjoy new flavors, smells and textures but a child learning to ignore these senses. What will happen when this child becomes a teenager and has to choose his own food and quantities? If his sense of hunger and satiety are lost, so is his ability to manage his food consumption in a healthy manner. Let your child learn to respond to his or her own needs. Trust them.

Deception

Many parents hide food in order to get their children to eat what they think is healthy. There are even several cookbooks that will assist you in these efforts. What does hiding food accomplish? On the positive side it allows parents to feel better about the healthy foods their child unknowingly eats. All other consequences are negative. First, a parent who needs to hide certain foods has already stopped being an effective parent. Parenting is teaching. Hiding is deceiving. There is no parenting expert that encourages parents to deceive a child.

Parenting is modeling best behavior. A parent should not be afraid of a child or of making an unpopular decision. Parenting is not a popularity contest. Hiding food keeps the child happy but is modeling dishonesty and giving power to the child. Who do you want in charge of your household, them or you?

Ah, but what about the nutritional gains the child is making? One can only hide a small amount of undesirable food without a child noticing. Remember, children have greater sense of smell and taste than adults. My sister told me her child said, "I smell vegetables" when given a piece of pizza after the vegetables were secretly taken off so she could have more plain cheese pizza.

So how much nutrition is in the two tablespoons of broccoli hidden in the tomato sauce? Wouldn't it be better if a child regularly saw broccoli, saw people eating and enjoying broccoli and eventually included broccoli in his regular diet? This acceptance of broccoli may not come for several years, but if a child learns to accept and eat broccoli his nutritional gain by age 18 will be vastly greater than the child who has been eating small hidden bites of broccoli. Furthermore, that child will continue to eat broccoli even when there is no one around to hide it in his food. Studies have shown that once a child realizes that a parent is anxious for them to eat a certain food, the acceptance of that food decreases. The more parents meddle with their children's eating, the more likely the chance a child will retaliate, with disordered eating habits or other behaviors.

How long do you think you can fool your child? By the time a child is in grade school, if not before, they are pretty savvy about what is going on in their environment. They will eventually find out that you have been hiding food and they may rightly feel they have been lied to. What are you going to say when they ask, "Mom, is there squash in this brownie?" Perhaps later in their teenage years they will think that lies for someone's "own good" are okay, or that deceiving their parents a little is not really lying. Developing trust between parent and child is essential for a long term relationship; don't blow it over a teaspoon of peas.

On a practical level, how long do you want to keep hiding food? It takes more time to cook and puree vegetables into some other casserole, sauce or dessert than it does to steam or stir fry the same foods, plus the time and effort to hide the actual cooking process from your children. Is it worth it? Go for the long term gains. Be a parent. Teach and model what you know is right. It might take longer and there might be some tears and yelling, but if you're in it for the long haul, you'll do it right.

Give Them a Fighting Chance

I am not against offering children foods that they are familiar with and like. At all meals or snacks, always serve at least one food that your child usually eats even if this is bread, rice, apple slices or milk. I say usually because our children's likes and dislikes can change at a moment's notice. A child who has joyfully eaten macaroni and cheese for lunch for the past six months may one day look down at it and say, "I don't like that," or the more offensive and surprising, "You know I don't like that." This usually happens after you have purchased a case of macaroni and cheese. They will most likely return to their love for macaroni and cheese at some inconvenient time in the future, perhaps after you give the case of food to the local food bank or eaten it yourself.

It is dinner time. You choose the food and put it on the table and it includes one food familiar and likeable to the child. Don't serve a certain food just for the child, even if it is. If you are putting apple slices on the table so your child will like at least one food, don't put them just on the child's plate, put them in a serving dish for everyone. If the child has not eaten in at least one and a half hours, he is hungry and motivated. To increase chances of your child trying new foods, keep it simple. If you are having pasta and sauce, don't add the sauce to all of the pasta, keep some plain. If a rice dish calls for mixing in parsley and peas; keep some plain and serve small bowls of plain peas and plain rice. Your child may eat both foods plain but not mixed together. When making meatloaf, keep some meat out of the mix and brown it separately. Like myself as a child, many children will eat ingredients of foods but not when they touch or are mixed with other foods.

I never make special foods for my children, but I do provide them a simple version of what I am preparing. After eating foods separately for a while, a child may also determine that it is safe to try them mixed, so you are gently moving toward food acceptance with this technique. I have seen this work, with my daughter and even with my son. As they learn to try (and even like) mixed foods they become more willing to take a chance with other foods. This is a process, but my own experiences and testimonials from other parents tell me it is well worth it for them and their children.

How much should your child eat from each food group at each meal? They will eat as much or as little as they want to eat. Remember the second rule? You should offer a variety of foods including fruits, vegetables, grains, animal proteins, vegetable proteins, and oils and fats over the course of the day. All food groups do not have to be represented at each meal or snack. If a child is interested in eating a large quantity of applesauce, let him or her. Another day the same child may not touch applesauce but may prefer pasta or cheese. Children, like adults, eat different quantities of foods on different days. Don't worry about getting your child to eat from all of the food groups at each meal, each day or each week. Look at their food consumption over the course of a month. Did they eat some whole grains, some fruit, vegetables, milk, meat or fish? It is likely they did. Over the month they may have consumed seemingly enormous amounts of food one or two days and then seemed to live on air for several days. This is all normal for a child who is in touch with their body and their feelings of hunger and satiety. As you allow only certain amounts of fun food, a child will be drawn to other foods and will meet her nutritional needs naturally. Her growth should be steady and her development healthy.

I have seen this work with my son. We call him an opportunistic eater, waiting to fill up only on the foods he is comfortable with. But after a day or two of waiting for cookies or white bread to appear, he readily accepts other healthy foods. Without him knowing, his body is letting him know that he needs some nutrition.

If you are consistent with this method and it does not work for you, it is possible that your child's behavior has little to do with hunger and sense of fullness. Some children don't eat because of negative sensory experiences of taste, texture or smell. Others continue to eat beyond satiety due to the positive sensory experiences of taste, texture and smell. If you believe this may be your child's situation it is best to speak with an occupational therapist specializing in these areas. Other children may not eat or overeat due to environmental factors at home, school, or at play. If this may be the case, specialists such as social workers, psychologists or psychiatrists are available for helping the child and the family.

The Rules

1. You decide what to offer and when.

2. Your child decides whether to eat or not, how much to eat, and what order to eat the offered foods.

3. Never punish, reward or bribe with food.

Meeting Nutritional Needs

Toddlers are at risk for iron deficiency if their diet is low in iron and/or vitamin C or if milk intake is too high. Iron can be found in meats, beans, molasses, dark green vegetables, baked potato with the skin and even figs (Fig Newton-type cookies do not count). Vitamin C (found in many fruits and some vegetables) enhances the absorption of iron. Calcium, found in milk products, can block the absorption of iron so try not to serve milk with a meat meal. Your child only needs two cups (16 ounces) of milk per day. This ensures enough calcium, vitamin D and meets 75% of their protein needs. More than three cups of milk per day may interfere with iron absorption and can also decrease the amount of solid food intake.

Milk – In all Its Various Forms

Milk. What does this word mean to you? It used to mean milk from a cow, homogenized and pasteurized. Now, milk may refer to beverages from soy, rice, almonds, oatmeal or other nondairy products. Additionally, milk products bear labels such as "nonfat,"

47

"low fat," "enriched," and "acidophilus added," not to mention flavors ranging from the old fashioned chocolate to the ever-present coffee.

Definitions

So how about a few definitions? *Homogenization* means that the cream (fat) particles of the milk are broken down into smaller pieces, allowing them to stay evenly dispersed in the milk, avoiding cream rising to the top. *Pasteurization* is heating the milk at a high enough temperature to kill off disease causing organisms. Therefore, young children and nursing mothers should never drink unpasteurized milk, referred to as raw milk. *Acidophilus* is good bacteria added to milk to help ease digestion. Flavored milks, both from cows or non-dairy sources, have the same nutrients, including protein and calcium, as their non-flavored partners; however, the flavoring usually adds sugar (calories). Coffee milk should be avoided for those wanting to avoid caffeine, although the amount is not great.

How Much Milk Per Day?

Before age one, a child should have either formula or breast milk and be fed on demand. After twelve months, whole milk is recommended until age two. At age two, whole milk can be continued or replaced with 2% milk. Nonfat milk (formerly skim) is not recommended as children need 30% of their calories from fat. Whole milk is 49% calories from fat, 2% milk is 35% calories from fat (it is 2% fat by weight), and nonfat has no fat. Nonfat milk may be appropriate of the teenager who needs the protein and calcium but does not want the calories from fat.

Milk is a source of protein, calcium and vitamin D, but it is not a whole food like formula or breast milk. Too much milk will not allow your child to be hungry for a variety of other foods, offering a variety of nutrients. Two cups of milk a day will provide a one to three year-old with all of his protein and calcium needs, and four to eight year-olds with 84% of their protein and 75% of their calcium requirements.

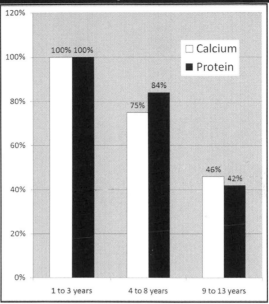

% of Protein and Calcium in Two Cups of Cow Milk

Concerns About Cow's Milk

Cow's milk is one of many sources of calcium, protein and Vitamin D. With just two cups per day a toddler will receive 100% of his calcium and protein needs; a preschooler will receive 75% and 84% respectively. So why is there a controversy about drinking milk? Is it the milk itself or substances given to the cows? Some people are concerned about the antibiotics and hormones (BGH=bovine growth hormone) that are routinely given to dairy cows to combat infection and increase milk production. Are these substances getting into our milk supply and if so, are there negative effects?

Some experts believe there is reason to be concerned but there have been no definitive studies. Organic milk is obtained from cows that do not receive antibiotics or hormones. These cows are also fed organic feed so they are not eating grains treated with pesticides. So if you are concerned, organic milk is an option as are organic non-animal milks.

There are a few small scientific studies linking cow's milk consumption to Type I diabetes in children predisposed to diabetes. In some children, too much milk may contribute to constipation or iron deficiency. Sometimes eczema will clear up in a child if milk is eliminated from the diet. Milk is also one of the top eight food allergens, but so are other common foods such as wheat and soy.

Some children experience diarrhea and/or gas and bloating after eating milk or other dairy products. This could be lactose intolerance. Lactose is milk sugar, which is naturally occurring in milk. If an individual's body is not producing enough of the enzyme (lactase) which breaks down this sugar into smaller easily digestible parts, it may cause gas, bloating and/or diarrhea. Lactose intolerance can be mild (moderate amounts of dairy can be digested) to severe (any dairy product causes symptoms). See your pediatrician or a dietician to help determine if there is lactose intolerance, and how to adjust dairy consumption and maintain sufficient calcium levels to best meet a child's health needs. If your child reacts to milk by vomiting, sudden skin irritations, breathing problems or severe diarrhea, you can suspect a milk allergy. If breathing problems or other severe symptoms occur, call 911 immediately. For other symptoms call your pediatrician or allergist.

If any of these issues concern you, you can avoid dairy products completely and get enough calcium from foods such as tofu, greens, instant oatmeal, figs, almonds, and ground sesame seeds. Many cold breakfast cereals and energy bars are now supplemented with calcium, as is orange juice. Calcium supplements are also available for children. Always check with a pediatrician or dietician before giving your child supplements.

Non Animal Milks

Non-animal milks such as soy, rice, almond, oat and others are usually nonfat or low fat, and are designed for the "health conscious" adult. For children, buy the product with the most calories from fat. To supplement the loss of fat in the milk you may want to add small amounts (1-2 teaspoons a day) of vegetable oils to your child's diet. (Try olive oil on bread, rice or veggies.) Only use non-animal milks if they are ENRICHED. This means that the product has added calcium, Vitamin D and other nutrients that make it equivalent to cow's milk. The protein in soy milk is similar to cow's milk. Other nondairy milks usually provide much less protein than cow milk. However, other protein foods can easily make up this difference. Make sure these are "enriched" to insure their vitamin and mineral equivalency to cow milk. Also check their fat, sugar and protein levels. Even with enrichment, except for soy, many of these products do not have similar protein levels as cow's milk. Soy and other nondairy milks should be shaken vigorously prior to pouring to insure that the added calcium has not sunk to the bottom of the container.

Cow Milk Product Substitutes

Another method for avoiding cow's milk products is by using soy yogurt, soy cheese and other nondairy substitutes. As soy contains phytoestrogen, a plant base compound similar to estrogen, there is concern by parents that too much soy may interfere with normal maturation, especially in boys. There appear to be no good studies proving this to be the case. Plant derived estrogen has just 1/100,000 the strength of steroidal estrogens. However, it is advised that soy supplements not be used as they contain very concentrated level of phytoestrogens not found in soy milks. Keep in mind that some nondairy cheeses do contain an ingredient called casein. This is a protein from cow milk. Casein will not affect those who are lactose intolerant, but will trigger a reaction to those who are allergic to cow milk.

Fruit Facts

Let's be clear, fruit is the once-living food that was harvested from a plant and is most often purchased in the produce section of the grocery store or from a farmers market. Fruit can also be spotted on the tree, vine or plant and picked and eaten as is. Fruit contains no human-added anything and is composed of carbohydrate and very little naturally-occurring protein or fat. All others products with fruit in the name are processed fruit, or contain some processed fruit in the manufacturing of the product.

Fruit Drinks and Juice

When purchasing juice, don't be fooled by the large lettering on the container proclaiming "made with real fruit juice." Any beverage that uses the word "drink" is not 100% juice. These drinks are usually made with very little real juice. The amount (usually 5%) is stated in very small letters on the nutrition label. However, most juice drinks are almost nutritional equivalents of 100% real fruit juice. A drink made with corn syrup or sugar contains comparable calories and carbohydrates (sugars) as real juice. There may be a few more nutrients in the real fruit juice, unless the fruit drink is enriched, but not many.

Does My Child Need Juice?

No. Although most of us consider juice a fruit, it is just the sugar and water from several pieces of fruit concentrated into a sweet and tasty drink. A half cup of orange juice has 3-6 teaspoons of sugar (14-18 grams of carbohydrate). The bulk of the fruit, including fiber and other nutrients, is not included. Orange juice does have vitamins B and C vitamins. Vitamins are added to many 100% juices to boost their nutritional value, but these juices are really just colorful sugar water. Half a piece or one cup of fresh fruit has ¾ to 2 ½ teaspoons of sugar (7-10grams of carbohydrate) plus fiber and a vast array of other nutrients. This is why our children do not need juice, except to help with occasional constipation. Offer juice to your child as you would a sweet dessert, occasionally and in small quantities.

A child who is allowed to have juice any time or all of the time may have increased incidence of tooth decay, a tendency towards diarrhea, and lack of interest in other foods. A child allowed to consume juice will have a sense of fullness and energy from juice's calories and will not feel hungry for solid food. A great way to keep your child from eating his or her lunch is to offer it with juice. However, solid foods provide the vitamins, minerals and fiber needed by children to grow strong bones, healthy bodies and alert minds. For these reasons, the American Academy of Pediatrics recommends a maximum of 4-6 ounces of juice per day.

As children become better chewers, dry fruit may be an option. Dry fruit travels well in diaper bags, cars and backpacks. However, many dry fruits have sugar added to sweeten, moisten or preserve the product. Again, look closely at the package label. Sold as a single ingredient, raisins almost never have added sugar whereas cranberries and bananas almost always do. Keep in mind that a child allowed to eat a lot of dry fruit should also be given fluids to aid in digestion; after all, dried fruit is fruit without the water.

Fruit Products

There are many products on the market that like to pass themselves off as fruit. These are products that display "fruit" in the name or prominently on the package, like fruit bars, fruit leather, fruity bears, and fruit snacks. Examples of these are cookies that advertise "no sugar added, only natural fruit juices," drinks that read "real fruit juice included" and "fruit drink." "Fruit juice" is usually concentrated fruit and nutritionally no different than sugar. The "real fruit juice included" may be as little as 5%. "Fruit drink" usually has no fruit in it. Also beware of products containing "real fruit." The fruit may be real, but how much fruit is actually in the product? Sometimes it is less than ½ a teaspoon per serving even though there are large, colorful pictures of fresh fruit on the package. To help determine how much fruit is in such a product, check out the ingredient list. As ingredients are listed from the highest quantity to least, where on the list is the fruit? Is it even in the list of ingredients?

When buying fruit bars, leather, or any gummy shaped "fruit" candy, check the ingredient label. If the first ingredient is sugar, corn syrup, honey, or any word ending in "ose" (glucose, fructose, sucrose) this is candy, not fruit, even if it is sold in the produce section.

Some of these fruit products are 100% fruit, like the ones my children have cajoled me into purchasing. These bars are 45 calories and contain 9 grams of sugar. As there are 4 grams of sugar in a teaspoon, and a teaspoon has 15 calories, 9 grams of sugar is about 33 calories. So the remaining 12 calories come from the other carbohydrate components of the fruit. By comparison, half a graham cracker or 1 cup of popcorn has less calories and only a negligible increase in fat. So even a 100% fruit product is mostly sugar, but the word "fruit" even makes me feel better.

Fruit Sweeteners

Some cookies, muffins, and other traditionally sweet products are sweetened with fruit juice or fruit concentrate. Fruit concentrate is fruit without its fiber, attached nutrients and water, leaving only sugar. Our bodies know that fruit concentrate is sugar and digests it as such. Is sugar extracted from fruit any healthier than sugar extracted from sugar cane? No, both are naturally growing plants.

My Child Won't Eat Vegetables

Many of you are concerned that your child does not eat enough vegetables. So, should you force-feed them, hide them in other foods, give up? Per the rules, I don't recommend any of these approaches. As with all foods, we should never force, bribe or reward a child to eat anything. This ultimately sends the wrong message: that food should be eaten to please someone else or to gain something else. Eating is about nourishing our bodies and knowing when we are hungry or satiated.

Try Again, and Again and Again. Repeat.

Offering vegetables on a regular basis along with other foods is the most productive way to help children include vegetables into their meals. You can encourage this choice by eating vegetables yourself and commenting on their positive qualities such as color, crunchiness, taste or shape.

Children may need to see foods 10-15 times before they decide to eat it, so don't give up after a few tries. I tell my children to put their dishes in the dishwasher several times a day. Sometimes they do it without a reminder, sometimes not. I hope that eventually they will just do it. It's the same with trying foods. Remember, your only job is to offer food, and their job is to eat it or not. Don't give up.

A child may eat hidden vegetables, but they may also notice them and refuse the food. This breaks a trust you have with your child. Do you want your child to be suspicious of the foods you offer? We all know that a child who unknowingly eats broccoli in spaghetti sauce will not accept steamed broccoli on its own. When you say, "You liked it in the spaghetti sauce," they feel betrayed and now they won't eat spaghetti sauce either!

Make Friends with Vegetables

Vegetables in any form are nutritious for your child, whether they're raw, frozen, canned or cooked. To make the most of your efforts, offer the orange-yellow vegetables like carrots, sweet potatoes, yams, squash and red and yellow peppers which contain the most nutrients per bite. The green leafy vegetables like kale, collards, spinach, broccoli, brussel sprouts and chard are also packed full of nutrients but difficult for most children. A baked potato, including the skin, is also very nutritious. Other vegetables with a high nutrient per bite ratio are peas, asparagus, avocado, green beans and corn. Purchase canned vegetables with no salt, low salt or with less than 20% of the daily value from sodium to avoid unwanted salt. Avoid frozen vegetables that come with sauce, especially cream sauce, as this usually adds too much salt and fat.

Beware of vegetable snack foods. Don't fool yourself into thinking that fried snack products such as puffed peas, potatoes or veggie chips are vegetables. The nutrient value in these products is not anywhere near that of real vegetables, and the fat and sodium make them a fun food, not one that helps a child grow big and strong.

Children are more likely to eat vegetables if they have some involvement with the food. Reading books about vegetables, planting a garden, picking vegetables from a farm, visiting a farmers market, and washing or preparing vegetables for the meal are all ways a child can experience the vegetable before they see it on the table. Children love to bake and eat the results. Try a carrot cake or zucchini bread recipe. Children also like choice. At the store, let them pick one or two vegetables to take home. At home let them choose one of two vegetables to have in their lunch.

For children under age two, raw vegetables can be choking hazards. Stir-frying, steaming, roasting and grilling vegetables are tasty method for cooking vegetables. Some children prefer vegetables they can hold in their hand and dip into sauces or dressings. Others need a little butter or salt, which is fine as long as it is used to enhance the flavor of the vegetable rather than the vegetable being used as a delivery device for sauces or condiments.

How Many Vegetables Should My Child Eat?

So how many vegetables does a child need per day? Per my second rule, as much as they are willing to eat. Offer a variety of vegetables throughout the day, maybe two to three different times. Let your child decide if he will eat them or not. If they don't eat any one day, they may eat them the next day or week. The nutrients in vegetables are also available in fruits, seeds, nuts and grains, so do not despair if they don't eat any. Serve, eat and enjoy.

The Vegetarian or Vegan Choice

What is a vegetarian diet? The strict definition is a diet that eliminates the flesh of any animal. This includes fish, shellfish, pork, beef, chicken, duck, elk, rabbit, venison and any other animal. A vegetarian diet does include products from animals such as milk products, eggs and honey. Someone who chooses not to eat any meat flesh or products from an animal is referred to as vegan. Both a vegetarian or vegan diet is appropriate for a child.

Sometimes children choose a vegetarian diet even before they know the word exists. Many infants reject meat. We don't know why this is, but most of them reverse this trend and start accepting meat before they are two years-old if it is regularly included in the family's diet. Sometimes a child comes to the realization that meat is a dead animal. The child may then choose not to eat meat out of sympathy, disgust or both. With some children this is temporary, with others it can be long lasting. Some children (and adults) call themselves vegetarian but make personal exemptions for specific food. Some self-proclaimed vegetarians will eat fish, perhaps not feeling as strongly about fish as land animals. When I declared myself a vegetarian as a teenager I continued to eat pepperoni on pizza, unwilling to give up a favorite food.

Regardless of why your child is not eating meat, for however long it lasts, their health does not have to be compromised. There are many health professionals that believe it is actually healthier not to eat meat. A healthy diet is one comprised of whole grains, fruits and vegetables, healthy fats and protein. Vegetarians and vegans eat all of these foods. The only nutrients that are more readily available in meat or animal products are protein, iron, calcium and B-12. There are plenty of protein sources available to vegetarians and vegans. Vegetarians have a few more choices than vegans as their diet allows for dairy products and eggs, both protein sources. See the chapter on "protein" for vegan and vegetarian sources of protein and adequate amounts.

Iron

Meat is a very useful source of iron as it is the most easily absorbed by the body. However, like protein, iron can be found in non-meat forms. A serving of beef has about 3-4 mg of iron per 3 ounce serving (a serving the size of a deck of card). The following are good non-animal and child friendly sources of iron:

Baked beans ½ cup	2.0 mg
Kidney beans ½ cup	2.0 mg
White bread 2 slices	1.4 mg
Enriched cooked noodles (1 cup)	1.9 mg
Frozen peas (cooked) ½ cup	1.3 mg
Prune juice ½ cup	1.5 mg
Raisins (not packed) ¼ cup	1.0 mg
Baked potato (with skin) ½	1.5 mg

For older children, after age 5, serve nuts and seeds for iron:

Almonds 1 oz.	1. 0 mg
Dry roasted cashews 1 oz.	1.7 mg
Dry roasted pistachios 1 oz.	1.2 mg
Roasted pumpkin seeds 1 oz.	4.24 mg
Roasted sesame seeds 1 oz.	4.19 mg

Iron from plants is not as easily absorbed as iron from animals. To help increase absorption, iron foods should be paired with foods high in vitamin C such as oranges, cantaloupe, strawberries, mango, and peppers. Cooking in a cast iron pan also increases iron in foods.

HOW MUCH IRON DOES MY CHILD NEED?		
Group	Age	Amount of Iron
Children	7-12 Months 1-3 Years 4-8 Years	11 mg 7 mg 10 mg
Males	9-13 Years 14-18 Years	8 mg 15 mg
Females	9-13 Years 14-18 Years	8 mg 15 mg

Calcium

A child vegetarian should have no problem receiving an adequate amount of calcium if they are regularly eating dairy products. For a vegan, the calcium must be found in other foods. Children ages 1-3 years need 500 mg. calcium, children ages 4-8 years need 800 mg, and children ages 9-18 need 1300 mg. A vegan child can obtain calcium from the following non-animal sources:

Enriched soy milk 1 cup	250 mg (varies)
Almonds 3 oz.	210 mg
Broccoli 2 stalks	250 mg
Tofu 3 oz.	110 mg
Dried figs 3 oz.	100 mg
1 package oatmeal	163 mg
Calcium enriched orange juice	varies
Calcium enriched breakfast cereals	varies

Vitamin B-12

Vitamin B-12, found primarily in meat, is also found in eggs and milk products. Therefore the elimination of meats as in a vegetarian diet should not affect this nutrient. However, vegans will need to supplement their diet with B-12 or eat foods processed with B-12. Several common breakfast cereals are enriched with this essential nutrient. If you choose to raise a vegan child, check with your health care provider to help select the appropriate amount of B-12 and to assure that your child's diet includes the appropriate amount of vitamins and minerals.

Chapter 3

EXCEPTIONS TO THE RULES

Snacks-Not Just Junk Food Time

Kids always seem to be eating, probably because they are. Most children need to eat every 1 ½ hours to 3 hours depending on their own personal rhythms. Of course, this means that we need to provide as many as six meals or snacks per day. If this seems daunting to you remember that many of these meals and snacks are quick and easy to prepare.

Meals and Snacks: Nutritional Equivalents

However, don't look at snacks as fun food give-away time. To children under the age of six there is really no difference between meals and snacks. Those under five don't know what time it is or what day it is so they certainly don't know that at breakfast, lunch and dinner they should eat more or healthier foods than at snack time. They just know that they are hungry. For all ages, meals and snacks should be of equal nutritional value. If meals and snacks are nutritionally equal, we're not mad, disappointed or frustrated if a child eats more during snacks and less at meals. We don't feel the added pressure to make sure they eat something healthy at the meals, as this has most likely occurred at a previous meal or snack. We can trust their rhythm of hunger and satiety and not override it due to the time on the clock.

Growing Food and Fun Food

Like meals, snacks should always contain an unlimited amount of "growing food" and, if you like, a limited amount of a "fun food". When including fun food say to your child, "This food is just for fun so we are only eating two pieces, but you can have as much banana as you would like. It is a growing food." At each meal or snack, a child should be permitted to eat until they reach satiety, or fullness, but not to fill himself from the fun food alone. If after eating all of the fun food offered they are still hungry, the child should be reminded that the growing food is still available. A child should be allowed to eat this food until they decide they have had enough to eat. Let your child learn the security of knowing that he will have enough food to satisfy him. Let your child stay in touch with his own innate ability to know when he is hungry and full.

An all-starch or carbohydrate snack such as apples and a bagel, or pretzels and grapes, will quickly supply a child with energy and just as quickly leave the child hungry again. To get mileage out of snacks (as well as meals), they should contain a carbohydrate food as well as some protein and/or fat. This is especially important for older children and teens who may not eat as often as younger children. For example, serve apples with cheese or yogurt and bagels with humus or deli meats. Pretzels could be served with nut butters and grapes with flavored tofu squares.

Here are 30 examples appropriate for children aged one year and older. I have not listed any serving sizes as we should let the child decide when they have had enough to eat.

30 Snack Suggestions

1. Animal crackers and low fat yogurt, water

2. Bagel and tofu spread, pineapple or nectarines, and water

3. Refried bean dip and pita bread wedges, water

4. Oyster crackers and nut butter, milk or water

5. Muffin and bean salad (from can or jar), water

6. Garlic bread and mozzarella cheese, kiwi, water

7. Teddy Grahams and pudding, bananas, water

8. Foccacia bread and avocado, water

9. Cooked, cold pasta and egg salad, water

10. Pumpkin bread and smoothie (milk, banana, frozen berries)

11. Pretzel sticks and bean dip, water

12. Zucchini bread or Chex cereal and milk

13. Whole wheat flour tortilla rolled with deli slices, water

14. Graham crackers, soy butter, plums, water

15. Melon, Rye Krisp crackers, cold previously cooked chicken, water

16. Hard breadsticks dipped in hummus, peas (frozen OK), water

17. Banana bread or Cheerios and milk

18. Salmon (canned) and english muffin, water

19. Fruit salad in soy yogurt and vanilla wafers, water

20. Cottage cheese and berries (fresh or frozen), water

21. Cold (steamed) broccoli and jicama sticks dipped in salad dressing, water

22. Hard boiled egg, peaches (canned or fresh), milk

23. Cold cheese tortellini and pears (canned or fresh), water

24. Mix: oyster crackers, small pretzels and Chex cereal with minestrone soup (unheated is okay) water

25. Raisin or cinnamon bread and yogurt, water

26. Baked beans, saltine crackers, water

27. Monterey jack cheese and bread stick, optional spaghetti sauce (for dipping), water

28. Applesauce (unsweetened) and crispy rice cereal, milk

29. Corn bread, string cheese and mandarin oranges or tangerines, water

30. Whole wheat roll and jelly, nut butter (sunflower), milk

Eating at Restaurants with Young Children

Just because you have children doesn't mean that you can no longer eat in a restaurant. The experience will definitely be different than pre-kids, but with some planning it can be enjoyable. Here are some suggestions from other parents who have taken their children to restaurants, and survived.

Survival Suggestions

✓ Go early for better service and avoid waiting for a table.

✓ Choose family restaurants.

✓ Choose noisy restaurants.

✓ Choose restaurants where children can be entertained: ceiling fans, fire places, fish tanks, open kitchens, and other babies can be helpful.

✓ After ordering, take children for a walk around the restaurant or outside.

✓ Make reservations if possible

✓ Order an appetizer as your child's meal.

✓ Share your meal with a child (don't need to order "kid's meal"). Ask for an extra plate.

✓ Let your child suck on a small lollipop while waiting for the food. The calories are negligible.

✓ Ask for what you want even if it's not on the menu.

✓ If eating at a food court or fast food restaurant, ask for everything "To Go" even if you are eating at the restaurant. You will receive your food without the tray and packed in a manner less likely to spill. The packaging will help keep the food warm as you purchase foods from different restaurants and get situated at a table.

How to Eat While the Food is Still Hot

✓   Take turns eating, one adult focusing on the children while the other one eats.

✓   Have you child's meal brought earlier (this may not work if the child finishes eating before you are done eating).

✓   Make sure your child is hungry so they, too, will be busy eating. Give only small amounts of snacks before the food arrives.

✓   Order something for the child that she likes, even if it is only French fries or rice.

✓   For a nursing baby, bring a pillow and nurse while you eat.

✓   Let the napping baby sleep in his carrier tucked under your table while you eat.

What to Bring

✓   Some of these items will make your meal much easier and therefore enjoyable. Don't be embarrassed to bring what you need.

✓   Portable high chair (upside-down wooden restaurant high chairs will hold some infant car seats)

✓   Floppy: a cloth with leg holes which fits over high chair and shopping cart

✓   Sippy cup

✓   A baby sticky mat with a catch flap

✓   Toys (on rings for babies)

✓   Small snacks to eat before food arrives or if child finishes first

✓   Food for an infant unable to eat table foods

✓   Disposable or reusable mat for table

✓   Bib

✓ Wipes

✓ Small games, toys, papers and crayons for older children

Safety

The restaurant does not have your child's safety as a primary concern, therefore it is up to you to assess the environment and make changes as needed to ensure your child's comfort and safety.

Possible Problems:

✓ Move table items out of child's reach before child sits down (knives, salt shakers, water glasses, etc).

✓ Make sure child can not pull the table cloth off.

✓ Don't put a cafeteria tray down within child's reach.

✓ Check food temperature.

✓ Check for hot plates, especially in Mexican restaurants.

✓ Check the cleanliness of table tops, highchairs and floor.

✓ Check the stability of restaurant chair or high chair.

✓ Check high chair for loose screws or other parts.

The Mess

Some children make messes while they eat. Don't let this totally discourage you from taking them out to eat. Here are some hints to deal with messes:

✓ Pick up after your child.

✓ Tip more. Don't forget the bus person, who is likely to do most of the cleaning.

✓ Use a bib with a catch pocket at the bottom.

✓ If available, ask for a paper drop cloth or bring one.

✓ Don't put too much food on your child's tray or plate.

Enjoy Yourself

Keep in mind why you are at a restaurant. If you want to enjoy yourself and the others at the table you may choose to let your child order something that is not the best choice nutritionally but will keep your child occupied and content. One evening out to dinner with my visiting parents I let my son order French fries, just French fries. That is all he said he wanted to eat. The French fries and all the food came. We all ate a leisurely dinner. There were no behavior problems, no disruptions, and no interruptions to adult conversation. Of course my parents gave me a hard time. How could I, a nutritionist, allow my child to eat only French fries for dinner? I told my parents that we don't eat out much, maybe one meal a week. I wanted to enjoy the evening and their company. My son is offered a variety of healthy and fun foods four to six times a day. A meal of French fries is a small price to pay for a good time at dinner.

Some children are just not good restaurant children. For success, go into a restaurant with the correct attitude. Know that you can always leave. If your child is not behaving appropriately, the restaurant staff will be more than happy to get you your check and quickly pack your food to go. Despite your proper parenting, it is hard for some children to eat out. For these children you may choose to order take out instead of going out. In good weather you can have a great take out picnic at your favorite park, beach or even in your own yard. If you do go out, try to choose a restaurant with very fast service and bring something for this child to do while she waits for food or for others to socialize after a meal. For extreme cases, there is always the babysitter.

Parties, Buffets and Other Free-For-Alls

Others Offering Your Children Fun Food

Despite your best parenting efforts, your children will be offered foods that you would not give them, and at times you would prefer them not to eat. This happens at the bank when the teller offers your one year-old a piece of hard candy (no thank you, that is a choking food), at play dates (once my three-year-old daughter was offered a 16 ounce glass of juice), or at a birthday party where everyone goes home with a bag of candy on top of the cake and ice cream just served at 5:00 pm. There are the holidays, especially Halloween, Valentine's Day and Easter, when candy seems to be central to the celebration. Let's not forget Christmas cookies and deep-fried potato pancakes called latkes served (with sour cream) at Chanukah. Then there are the nice people at the grocery store handing out samples and telling your child to "take a few." Where I live, people in parades regularly throw candy to the crowd, causing children to leave their parents and throw themselves into the street to wrestle the treats from other children. Have you ever found out that a babysitter was bribing your children with candy or a trip to some fast food restaurant despite your request that they not? (The babysitter won't say anything but the kids will slip up eventually.) Even our own parents sometimes work against us. They believe it is their right to spoil the grandchildren. Who are we to argue?

It is hard to escape others wanting to give our children "treats." They want to do something nice for our children. Everyone loves to see a child's face light up with a smile. What better way to bring it out than with some fun food? Many treats at holidays and parties are part of our family traditions or religious celebrations. Food, culture and good times are very inter-twined. So how does a parent handle all of this wealth of generosity, kindness and inclusion?

Parents have found a variety of ways to help a child make the right choice or to lessen the amount of fun foods offered. When your child is given a large amount of candy at one time you may choose to not let them keep all of it. Until my children were eight they got to keep as many pieces as their age. We stopped at eight as that seemed like enough to me; you can choose the number you think is right for your child. Once the candy is home, they leave it in the kitchen and can have one piece a day. Some people let their children eat as much as they can the day they receive it and then throw the rest out. This usually leads to children eating more than is right for their bodies. Even with fun food, children should take their time with eating and stop when they are full. They will do this if they know that there will be other fun food opportunities later in the week and in their lives.

Each time a child is offered food by someone else the circumstances will be different. If the food item offered is small you may just let them eat it and not worry about it having any effect on the next meal. If it is a large amount of food you may ask that it be saved until the meal. You may also decide to let the child have the food.

When younger children see other children eat they want to eat as well, usually the foods the others are having. This can be a difficult situation especially if you don't want your child to eat at this time. You have several choices, none detrimental to your child. You can feed your child, you can tell your child they have to wait until later, or you can leave the area of the eating children. If you want to stay you may have to offer food and just accept that they may not eat much at the next meal or snack, or you may delay the next meal or snack for when the child will be hungry again. Be flexible; in some circumstances it may not be polite, culturally or socially, to decline the food. If so, just enjoy the moment.

Holidays and Traditions

Certain foods are only offered once a year, especially those related to holidays and other traditions. These are times to enjoy the celebration and the associated foods. Rainy days are great times to stay home and make brownies. Children love making and eating fun food with you. You can moderate consumption by letting your child know that these are fun foods and set a limit on the amount they can have at the time.

When Halloween candy becomes excessive there are two plans I have used successfully. One involves the Great Pumpkin. Tell your child that on Halloween night the Great Pumpkin comes out looking for candy to trade for toys. After you child chooses a small number of candy to keep, have them place the rest of the candy outside. Like the Tooth Fairy, the Great Pumpkin will come while they are sleeping, take the candy and leave a small surprise, like a small toy car or package of markers. As a child becomes older they may go along with this for the present. Another idea is to take the candy, buy some graham crackers and canned frosting and build a gingerbread house. Leave it around until Thanksgiving and then throw it away. I have a friend whose sons prefer to keep the gingerbread houses until July 4th and then blow them up.

Potty Training Awards

What about using fun food as a potty training reward? I am not a potty training expert but food should not be used as a reward or bribe. That said, even I went against my own advice and was desperate enough to offer candy to encourage potty use for my son. I learned my lesson; it didn't work even though he has an intense sweet tooth. My advice as a nutritionist and an experienced mother is to try other methods first. Small rewards such as colored markers, little toy cars, colored tape, pads of paper or stickers may work just as well. If you feel like you need to reward with a larger item or outing, use a chart. When the child uses the potty enough to fill in the chart, they receive the item or outing. Jan Faull, a potty training expert has written *Mommy! I Have To Go Potty* and her book can answer other potty-related issues.

Birthday Treats

Many of you will be asked to bring birthday treats to share with your child's classmates to celebrate your child's birthday. A party is a great time to share fun food with friends. However, if you would like to share foods that are somewhat healthier I have a few suggestions:

✓ Bread - A really good one, maybe with raisins or cinnamon. Some children enjoy warm garlic bread.

✓ Smoothies - Make some ahead of time or bring a blender and make them in the classroom. In the winter you can use canned pineapple, frozen berries, frozen mango and bananas.

✓ Popsicles- Buy whole fruit popsicles; kids love them even when it's cold outside.

✓ Warm Apple Cider (pasteurized) - Bring in a thermos of warm cider and serve with apple pie or graham crackers.

✓ Popcorn - For children older than age three.

✓ Frozen Bananas- Simply peel and cut ripe bananas in ½. Put a popsicle stick in the flat end and freeze on a cookie sheet. Before freezing you can roll them in chocolate jimmies.

✓ Egg rolls - Most kids like to dip these in sauce and eat.

✓ Bring in Cheerios, small pretzels, Fruit Loops and string. Have the children make edible necklaces.

✓ Fruit sorbet – serve in ice cream cones.

✓ Oatmeal cookies - Buy the ones that have oatmeal listed as the first ingredient.

✓ Really big soft pretzels.

✓ Chocolate chip bagels.

✓ Fortune cookies.

Eating at School

A packed lunch eaten away from home offers your child a certain amount of independence. The child can eat as much or as little as she chooses and the foods in the order she chooses. This freedom should exist for a child at each meal. Sometimes parents don't want a child to have this freedom so they tell the child or child's teacher to "make sure Alice eats her sandwich before she eats her chips and cookie." This is putting the teacher in a difficult situation. We all want our children's teachers to have strong trusting relationships with our children. We want them to let our children display their creativity, learn to be appropriately social and develop their intellectual strengths to their fullest. Then we ask them to tell our children how to eat and how much to eat, implying that the child can not be trusted. Children pick up on this, and this expectation is not fair to the teachers. If you don't want your child to eat the cookie before the sandwich, don't pack the cookie. Pack only healthy foods and then you won't be concerned about which foods your child eats.

The other side of this scenario is the teacher who takes it upon herself to tell your child what to eat and in what order. If this is the case, please let the teacher know you are fine with the child eating whatever food they want in whatever order they choose. I tape a note on or in my child's lunch box if this request is not honored.

Buffets

Buffets can be tricky for some parents but great fun for children. At home you offer certain foods to your child and let them to decide what to choose. At a buffet all foods are offered, including some that you would not choose. You have several ways to handle this situation. You can just give your child free choice, reminding them not to take more than they can eat. If they just pick carrot sticks and cake so be it. You can also limit fun food to certain amounts. If they only want dessert you can let them have it right away, or ask that they wait until everyone else is choosing dessert. During the wait they may find something else that they like to eat. You can also ask them to pick one healthy food and one fun food. But once they have done this you need to let them decide how much they will eat and in what order the food is eaten. I am at buffets so rarely with my children that I let them choose and eat what they want. They eat what they choose, I don't have to play the food police, and I get to enjoy my food as well.

Freedom to choose their food is a skill that children learn just as they learn independence from us. Children will make mistakes along the way, but this is part of the learning process. You will have to find your own way to balance your desire to offer a healthy diet and let your child enjoy the healthy and fun foods of celebrations, parties, holidays and buffets.

I have seen other parents observe me allowing my son to eat only dessert at buffets. I keep in mind that I am trying to teach my son to learn that his body needs foods that will help him grow big and strong but that fun foods are okay, too. My goal is to teach him to become aware of what his body needs no matter what that looks like to others.

Chapter 4

KNOW WHAT FOOD TO BUY

Carbohydrates

We all talk about carbohydrates, but what are they really? Carbohydrates are plant molecules that are used by our bodies as our primary source of energy. They work with proteins and fats to keep our bodies healthy. Carbohydrates can be broken down into three categories; most plant foods are a combination of all three.

Sugar

The first category is sugar, which includes simple and complex sugars. Simple sugars do not need any further digestion; they can move directly into the bloodstream and provide energy to the body. This group includes fruit sugars, table sugar, honey, brown sugar and some fruits and vegetables. Complex sugars are those that are made up of two or more connected simple sugars. These include maple syrup, molasses, dairy products and some fruits. Both simple and complex sugars are used by the body for quick energy.

Starch

The second category of carbohydrates is starch, which is sometimes referred to as a complex carbohydrate. Starches break down more slowly than simple sugars and are therefore helpful in keeping blood sugar steady. A steady blood sugar level keeps body energy at an even pace throughout the day. Foods that contain starches include whole wheat, brown rice, quinoa, corn, oatmeal, potatoes, and beans.

Fiber

The last category of carbohydrates is fiber. Fiber is mostly in-digestible but it still plays an important role in our health. This indigestible fiber is thought of as roughage; it passes through our digestive tract working as an internal scrub brush, keeping our digestive track clean. The other kind of fiber, soluble fiber, is made up of plant components that attract water and become gel-like. This gel-like substance slows down the rate at which food moves through our digestive tract, thereby slowing the rate at which sugar enters our blood stream. This helps keep blood sugar levels even. It also aids in elimination.

The Mayo Clinic recommends 19 grams of fiber for children two to three, and 25 grams for children four to eight years-old. Many countries consume diets much greater than those levels of fiber and these countries tend to have less diabetes, heart disease, and some cancers than in the United States. So, fiber is not harmful as long as your child receives plenty of fluids, fats and a variety of foods

How Much Carbohydrate Does a Child Need?

How much carbohydrate does your child need? Carbohydrate should make up 50% of your child's diet. The other 50% should be comprised of 30% fat and 20% protein. For a child eating 1200 calories per day, this would be 600 calories or 150 grams from carbohydrates (6 servings or 25 grams per serving). A 25 gram serving is approximately one-half of a bagel, 2 slices of bread, three-quarters cup of noodles, one-half cup baked beans, a banana, or 6 ounces of juice.

Some Carbohydrates are Better than Others

When choosing carbohydrate foods for your child, stay away from those with sugar as a first ingredient. Breakfast cereals with 7 grams or less of sugar per serving are low-sugar. White rice, white bread and pastas are less nutritious than the whole wheat brands. Most crackers, pretzels and puffed snack foods are very low in fiber and nutrients. They are fun foods and should not be used as a staple of a child's diet. Popcorn (for children over age three), oatmeal, and cereals and crackers with whole wheat are whole grain foods. When buying cookies, make sure the first ingredient isn't sugar but a grain, such as wheat, oatmeal, or rice.

When looking for a whole grain or whole wheat food, check the nutrition label for grams of fiber and the ingredient list. Don't be fooled by the loaf of bread in the brown plastic bag called Health Country's Finest Wheat Bread, even if the bread is brown in color (this can come from caramel or other artificial coloring). For a product to be whole grain, the grain will be the first ingredient and listed as such, for example, "whole wheat flour." Wheat flour is not whole wheat flour. This only tells you that the grain in the product is wheat.

Enriched wheat is also not whole wheat. Enriched wheat is whole wheat that has been stripped of its outer coating of bran, vitamins and minerals, and then enriched with iron and B vitamins. Nineteen vitamins and minerals are taken out of white enriched bread and five (riboflavin, niacin, B1, iron, and folate) are added back in when the bread is enriched. However, whole wheat bread has 44% more calcium, 75% more protein and 52% more healthy fat than white bread, plus thirteen other vitamins and mineral not in white bread that are important to overall health. The nutrients in whole wheat bread are naturally occurring; they are part of the grain, not added through processing and food technology.

If at first you or your children don't like the taste or texture of whole grain foods, give them a chance to grow on you. Try another brand of that food. They are all different. Mixing white and brown rice together is a great way to incorporate whole grains into your diet. Try old-fashioned oatmeal on a cold winter morning. Some children like sandwiches using a slice of white bread and a slice of whole wheat bread because of the color change. Cut this sandwich in quarters and make a checkered board pattern for the most fun and interest. Tortillas also come in whole wheat and can be wrapped around luncheon meats, tuna or even peanut butter and jelly.

Fruits and vegetables are also carbohydrates. To ensure you're receiving the most nutrition possible, eat these in their most natural form. Even juice from 100% fruit is processed. You are getting only the sugar and water from the fruit and throwing away the fiber and many nutritionally valuable parts of the plant. Plus, eating fruit leads to a greater level of satiety or fullness than juice.

Protein: The Newest Health Food?

With The Zone and other low carbohydrate diets still popular, many people see protein as the answer to their weight and nutrition needs. A high protein diet may produce weight loss results in the short term, but I do not recommend it as a maintainable diet and it's certainly not for infants or children. Protein has its place in our diets, but so do foods with carbohydrates, fats and oils. Any diet that omits a major food group is not a healthy diet. It will certainly be deficient in some necessary nutrients. A child should never be put on a high protein diet unless under the direction or care of a doctor. By eating only protein, you and your child will miss out on many essential and important nutrients.

How Much is Enough?

So how much protein do we need? The average man needs 60 grams of protein; the average woman and pre-teen need 45 grams. Children need 13 grams at age one and 34 grams by age ten. These protein levels will contribute about 10% of total daily calories.

The recommended dietary allowance for protein is as follows:

Age 1-3 = 13 grams

Age 4-8 = 19 grams

Age 9-13 = 34 grams

(Institute Of Medicine, 2005)

It is fairly easy to consume your daily minimum of protein if you have consistent access to food. Most of us eat more than we need without even thinking about it. A portion of meat or poultry (3 ounces), equal to the size of a deck of cards, and has 21 grams of protein. The equivalent of two thirds of a deck of card would meet all of a child's (ages one through three) daily protein needs and almost all of a child four to eight. Without eating a pure protein food, children can easily meet their dietary needs. A one-year-old will receive all of his or her protein needs in two cups of milk (4 grams per ½ cup). A five-year-old who doesn't drink any milk can achieve his or her protein needs (19 grams) over the course of the day by eating:

1 ounce of meat (7 grams)

½ cup yogurt (6 grams)

2 ounces of dry cereal (4 grams)

1 slice bread (2 grams)

other food is needed to meet caloric and other nutritional needs

Many people are successful on a protein diet because by increasing their protein, they feel hungry less often during the day. Protein does not leave our digestive tract as quickly as carbohydrate foods so protein does help us to eat less during the course of a day. Therefore, for children, as well as adults, remember to include a small amount of protein at every meal or snack along with a moderate amount of a carbohydrate food. One half of a bagel with an ounce slice of mozzarella cheese is approximately 165 calories and 10 grams of protein. A whole bagel is about 165 calories and 6 grams of protein. However, a child will feel full longer after eating cheese and half of a bagel due to the added proteins and fats.

The consumption of too much protein can cause our bodies to loose valuable calcium and fluid. When proteins are digested, the excess nitrogen produced needs to be flushed from the digestive system. This requires a lot of water. Without enough liquid, the body will draw water from the blood, leading to dehydration. Furthermore, this kidney-flushing also takes calcium with it. So, too much protein can lead to a decrease in the body's available calcium and fluid.

Animal Protein

If you enjoy meats, keep portions small (remember the deck of cards) and eat no more than two servings per day. For children, half of a deck of cards (1.5 ounces) one to two times a day is enough. Animal protein foods such as meats, eggs, and full fat dairy products can be high in saturated fats and cholesterol. These are the fats that can lead to heart disease and stroke. High red meat consumption has also been correlated to a higher risk of colon cancer.

Vegetable Protein

Vegetable proteins, such as nuts, seeds and beans, are much healthier because they are high in poly- or monounsaturated fats, which can help lower cholesterol and avoid diseases of the vascular system. Where as animal proteins contain no fiber, plant proteins-especially beans-have a high amount of fiber.

Sources of Protein	Grams
Cooked Spaghetti 1 cup	8
Peanut butter 2 T.	8
Peanuts 3 T.	7
Beef 1 oz.	7
Poultry 1 oz.	7
Fish 1 oz. or ¼ cup tuna	8
One Egg	7
Cheese (cheddar) 1 oz.	7
Cottage cheese ¼ cup	7
Cooked dry beans ½ cup	7
Yogurt ½ cup	6
Peas (boiled) ½ cup	4
Broccoli 1 cup	4
Milk ½ cup	4
Tofu ¼ cup	4
Breakfast cereal 1 oz.	2
Bread 1 slice	2
Asparagus ½ cup	2
Cooked cereals ¼ cup	1.5
Grapes or black berries 1 cup	1

Let's talk about fat. Or do I mean oil? Cholesterol? Partially hydrogenated saturated fat? It's confusing isn't it? Let's define some terms and then put them into a nutritional perspective.

Animal Sources

Fats can come from either animal or plant sources. Examples of animal fats include lard, shortening, butter, cheese, cream, eggs and red meats. These are usually solid at room temperature because they are chemically saturated; all possible links between chemicals are made. To visualize saturation think of your favorite shopping mall parking lot the day before Christmas. All of the parking spaces are taken- the lot is congested and saturated. Saturated fats are unhealthy as they tend to cause vascular congestion, which leads to heart.

Most animal fats contain cholesterol. Cholesterol is not a fat, but a waxy substance that is essential for the manufacturing of Vitamin D and many hormones, so it is not all bad. Cholesterol is divided into the "bad" cholesterol know as Low Density Lipoproteins (LDLs) and the "good" cholesterol know as High Density Lipoproteins (HDL). LDL cholesterol leaves waxy deposits in your arteries. Excess ingestion of saturated fats raises LDL cholesterol, possibly leading to cardiovascular (heart and veins) disease. To lower LDLs, limit saturated fats and increase fiber in your diet. HDL moves cholesterol deposits back to the liver to be broken down and used in other ways by your body. HDLs can be raised through aerobic exercise and an increase in specific plant oils.

Plants Sources

Plant fats are usually referred to as oils as they are liquid at room temperature. Examples of these oils include olive, canola, corn, flax seed, and soy. Plants that contain high amounts of oils include avocados, olives, nuts, and seeds. Plant oils or plant sources of food (fruits, beans, vegetables, grains) contain no cholesterol and very little saturated fats.

Plant oils are largely made up of polyunsaturated and monounsaturated oils. To visualize polyunsaturated vegetable oil, think about the parking lot at the mall at 10:30 am on a weekday in any month but late November through December. Some of the parking spaces are taken, but there are more available than not. The parking lot at 7:30 am, when only a few employees are parked, is like the monounsaturated vegetable oil- most of the spaces are open. Chemically, almost none of the bonds are made. An increase in polyunsaturated and monounsaturated fats can help to lower LDLs.

Partially Hydrogenated Saturated Fats

So what are partially hydrogenated saturated fats? They are vegetable oils that have been chemically altered and are sometimes referred to as trans fats. By using a chemical process, hydrogen is added to a mono- or poly-unsaturated fat, creating bonds where none existed. To understand this, think about the parking lot again. Take an empty or near empty lot and fill it (by adding hydrogen) until no spaces are left. This creates a saturated fat from a previously mono- or poly-unsaturated fat. The food product is still animal-fat-free, but partially hydrogenated vegetable oils are as unhealthy as saturated animal fats. Remember, saturated fats are those that lead to fatty build up in arteries. You will find these fats in cookie, crackers and snack products, many which claim to be from 100% vegetable oils. So beware of these oils.

Why do food manufacturers use these fats? First, partially hydrogenated saturated fats are solid at room temperature; cookies, crackers and other snacks are less likely to break, crack or chip during packaging and transportation. They will maintain their exact shape. Also, partially hydrogenated saturated snacks are chemically more stable; the fats will not go rancid as happens with less saturated vegetable oils. This ensures a longer shelf life. Since manufacturers are now required to list grams of trans fats, many have removed them. However, if they are replaced with saturated fats, the product is really not any healthier. All fats have the same amount of calories. A gram of fat, both animal and plant, is 9 calories. A gram of protein or carbohydrate is 4 calories. So, fats and oils are concentrated calories. This is why a pound of carrots are extremely less caloric than a pound of meat or nuts. Fats and oils are also the last parts of ingested food to leave your stomach, providing long-lasting energy. Think how long you feel full from a meal of fried fish, french fries and a milk shake.

But this lasting power of fat can also be used to your advantage. Eat a small amount of fat (preferably vegetable) at each meal and you will feel sated longer and need to snack less often. This leads to a daily decrease in calories.

Fats and Disease

Unfortunately, children are starting to show signs of too much saturated fat. This is not only seen by an increase in childhood obesity, but by high cholesterol, triglicerides (fats) and LDLs in blood. Long term, this can have serious medical effects such as high blood pressure, diabetes type II and cardio vascular disease, and not in old age but also in early or middle adulthood. So choose your fats and oils carefully and enjoy them in moderation.

Label Reading: What Does It All Mean

Definitions

Buying healthy food is not always as easy as one may think. Marketers have all sorts of techniques to get us to buy foods that we believe are beneficial due to misleading labeling. There are packaging banners such as "low fat," "no cholesterol," "reduced sodium," and most recently, "no trans fats." What do these words really mean? Some of these terms are actually regulated by the government; others are not and can be used freely.

Any food that uses the term "reduced" or "less" in regards to calories, sugar, cholesterol, sodium or fat must have at least 25% less of that item than the regular brand as regulated by law. For example, if the regular brand of soup has 1000mg of sodium (about 50% of your daily maximum), the reduced brand can have 750mg, which is 25% less but still about 40% of your daily maximum, hardly a low salt food. So, do the math: is "reduced" really a healthy choice? Many times it isn't. A healthier choice is labeled "low" or "very low." These terms are regulated by portion size to provide a moderate amount of sugar, fat or sodium. Also, be aware that when an ingredient is taken out, like salt or fat, another is usually added to keep the product's taste consumer-friendly. A reduction of fat sometimes means an increase in sugar.

Trans Fats

As of January 1, 2006, package nutrition labels are required to list trans fats in addition to saturated fats. Remember, the trans fats (aka partially hydrogenated saturated fats) are vegetable fats with all hydrogen attached so the fat acts, looks and tastes like saturated fats. These trans fats are as problematic, if not more so, than saturated fats to your health. This has prompted marketers to advertise "ZERO TRANS FATS" on many food products in hopes that consumers will believe that the food is either low in fat, low in unhealthy fats, or perhaps, good for them. This is only true if two criteria are met. First, is the product also free of saturated fat? Keep in mind that even 3 grams of saturated fat is 15% of your maximum allowable level per day and saturated fats are those that can contribute to several chronic diseases. Secondly, a product can be labeled "Zero Trans Fats" if a single serving (serving size is designated on the nutrition label) has .5 mg per or less per serving. If you are going to eat more than one serving of this product, it is no longer "trans fat free."

Decoding the Nutrition Label

So what to look for on the nutrition panel? First, notice that all of the nutrition information is listed for a portion of the food, not the whole bottle, can or package. A small frozen pizza may have 380 calories, but if you look at "Servings per Container" on the second line, it may list two servings. This means that there are 760 calories in the whole pizza. If you eat about 2000 calories a day, that is over 30% of your daily need. Add the 200 calories in a can of soda and you are halfway to your daily caloric needs.

The third line of the nutrition label lists calories and calories from fat in one serving size of the food. As a general rule, keep the fat calories at or below 30% of all calories per serving. If a food is 100 calories per serving, then more than 33 calories from fat would be considered a high-fat food. If that same food had 10 calories from fat, or 10% of calories from fat, it would be a low-fat food.

The next lines list "% Daily Values" (DV) for fats, sodium, carbohydrates, proteins and some key vitamins and minerals. The DV is based on a 2000 calorie diet. So a sodium DV of 35% lets you know that one serving of that food contains 35% of the

80

maximum amount of sodium a person eating 2000 calorie a day should consume. To use these numbers, remember that 5% DV or less is a good goal for ingredients you want to avoid or limit, like sodium, cholesterol, saturated and trans fats. Use a 20% DV as the upper-most limit for these substances. For substances that you want to increase such as vitamin A, vitamin C, calcium, fiber and iron, look for DVs above 5%.

Next on the list is carbohydrate. Carbohydrate includes fiber as well as sugar. High fiber is good for digestion and overall good health. Sugar includes naturally occurring sugar in grain, fruit, vegetables and even dairy products, as well as added sugars in any form (honey, fruit concentrate, fructose, maple syrup, brown rice syrup, etc). Sugar amounts are listed in grams. Keep in mind that 4 grams of sugar equals one teaspoon of sugar. If you saw someone put more than 2 cubes of sugar in a cup of coffee or tea, would you think that was too much? If sugar was listed in teaspoons rather than grams, would you buy juice that has 7 or 8 teaspoons of sugar? Check out sugar amounts on juices, sodas, yogurt and other non-dessert foods such as tomato sauce and ketchup. You may be surprised.

Nutrition Facts

Serving Size 1 cup (228g)
Servings Per Container 2

Amount Per Serving

Calories 260   Calories from Fat 110

	% Daily Value*
Total Fat 12g	18%
Saturated Fat 3g	15%
Trans Fat 3g	
Cholesterol 30mg	10%
Sodium 470mg	20%
Potassium 700mg	20%
Total Carbohydrate 31g	10%
Dietary Fiber 0g	0%
Sugars 5g	
Protein 5g	

Vitamin A	4%
Vitamin C	2%
Calcium	20%
Iron	4%

* Percent Daily Values are based on a 2,000 calorie diet. Your Daily Values may be higher or lower depending on your calorie needs.

		Calories:	2,000	2,500
Total Fat	Less than		65g	80g
Sat Fat	Less than		20g	25g
Cholesterol	Less than		300mg	300mg
Sodium	Less than		2,400mg	2,400mg
Total Carbohydrate			300g	375g
Dietary Fiber			25g	30g

Understanding the Ingredient List

The ingredient list on a food product can give you information that the nutrition panel does not. This information is of particular importance if anyone in your family needs to avoid a specific food or additive. The ingredient label lists the individual foods in the product in descending order by weight. So, if you are looking for a food that is a whole wheat product, the first ingredient should be *whole wheat flour*. If whole wheat flour is not the first ingredient, then the product may not meet your requirements. Check the first ingredient when choosing cookies or cereals. If the first ingredient is sugar, corn syrup, fruit juice concentrate or another sweetener, then this product is closer to candy than a grain-based food.

Keep in mind that some ingredients may not be listed in simple terms. All ingredients ending in *ose* are some type of sugar: think glucose, fructose, maltose, sucrose, etc. Ingredient labels also list the type of fat or oil in a product. Remember that vegetable oils are healthier than animal (saturated) fats. Animal fats are sometimes referred to as lard. Tropical oils such as palm and coconut are also saturated. Partially hydrogenated vegetable oil is a vegetable oil modified to act like an animal fat and is as unhealthy as saturated fats.

Ingredients That are Equal to Sugar

✓ Corn syrup

✓ Concentrated fruit juice

✓ Honey

✓ Brown sugar

✓ Brown rice syrup

✓ Maple syrup

✓ Fructose, lactose, glucose, maltose, dextrose

✓ Sucinat

✓ Molasses

There has been some legislation to require that manufacturers use common names for food ingredients or additives. (Additives are substances added to foods to enhance flavor, texture, or freshness.) An example of an unfamiliar ingredient is *casinate*. It should be followed by the word milk or milk protein to clarify its meaning. Agar and/or guar gum is often seen in imitation ice cream products. It is the gel like substance harvested from seaweed used to give low fat ice-cream a creamy, smooth texture and is perfectly healthy to consume. For a full list of unfamiliar ingredients or food additives check http://www.cspinet.org/reports/chemcuisine.htm. This is the site of the Center for Science in the Public Interest. It is a non-profit group which explains nutrition and food questions in plain English.

Dates on Food

In addition to the nutrition panel and the ingredient list, many foods have various date stamps. An *expiration date* tells you the last date the food is considered safe to eat. A *pull date* is the last date at which the product can be sold. The product is safe to eat past this date but the consumer may or may not be given an *expiration date*. Sometimes a product has a *packed on* date. This only gives the date of packaging and may or may not be helpful in deciding the freshness of a product. Other products have a *best if used by* date, which states the last time a product is considered optimal, but it may be consumed after this date.

Organic Food Products

Many people with young children wonder if the price of organic products is "worth it." I can't make that decision for you, but I can help you understand what "organic" is and is not.

Definition

Organic foods are grown without the use of genetic engineering, radiation, sewage sludge, or synthetic pesticides. Organic animals must be fed only organic feed, be given outdoor access and not be given antibiotics. Organic milk is from cows that meet all of the above criteria and are not given Bovine Growth Hormone (BGH). There are studies showing that organic products have more nutritional value than others, but there are also studies that show that they don't.

Products labeled 100% Organic contain only organic ingredients. A product labeled organic must have at least 95% organic ingredients. Washington, California and Oregon, as well as several others states, have had organic standards for many years. There is now a federal organic standard: the symbol is a circle with the words "USDA ORGANIC" stacked in black type.

Are Organic Foods More Nutritious?

There are no good studies on the health effects of pesticides on children. Our government has set some upper limits for some pesticides, but these are for adults. We do know that young children (infant – three years-old) take in more food per pound of body weight than adults because children are in an extremely rapid growth period. We also know that young children's immune systems are still developing and strengthening. For these reasons, some people choose to use organic products when their children are young. There are also some studies that reveal higher amounts of nutrients in organically grown produce. This is due to farming practices that differ from non-organic farming.

To help you make a decision I recommend "Food News", produced by a nonprofit called Environmental Working Group (EWG). Their web site is www.foodnews.org. Their current list of foods with the most and least pesticides may help your shopping decisions. The EWG claims that by avoiding their "dirty dozen" you can avoid 90% of pesticides. So avoiding these 12 products or buying them organically can alleviate guilt and lessen pesticide consumption. This compromise can also save the money and time that may be involved in purchasing all organic products.

From the Environmental Working Group Web Site:

12 Foods With Most Pesticides	
Peaches	Cherries
Apples	Lettuce
Sweet bell peppers	Grapes (imported)
Celery	Pears
Nectarines	Spinach
Strawberries	Potatoes

12 Foods With Least Pesticides	
Onions	Avacado
Pineapples	Sweet corn (frozen)
Mango	Sweet peas (frozen)
Kiwi	Asparagus
Bananas	Cabbage
Eggplant	Broccoli

It takes time to be an informed consumer. Keeping our selves and our families safe and healthy is hard work. The reward is seeing our children grow into healthy teens and adults.

Chapter 5

EFFICIENT SHOPPING, QUICK COOKING AND ENJOYABLES MEALS

Family Meals

With the birth of the first child come many changes. Parents' daily activities and schedules shift from taking care of self to taking care of another. Meals that may have been either scheduled or makeshift take on a new appearance. At first all may seem calm, as the baby is either taking a bottle or breastfeeding. Bottle or breastfeeding is usually done apart from meal times so parents have their hands free to feed themselves. When the child is ready for solids, many parents will continue to feed the child before or after the adult meal so that they themselves can eat. Furthermore, as baby's first foods are generally different than parent meals, it seems to make sense to prepare the baby's meal away from adult meals.

Family Meals Defined

So what is a family meal? One mother I recently spoke with was concerned that her husband was rarely home for dinner; however, they did eat all breakfasts together, as well as all weekend meals. I assured her that the meal which you eat as a family is not as important as eating as a family. The meal time does not matter. In the predominant culture in the U.S., dinner is usually the family time. However, some cultures focus on a long leisurely lunch time for families to be together. The goal is to be together, without the television, radio, computer or reading materials to distract people from each other. (One study showed that watching television negates many of the positive outcomes of family meals.) It is a time for everyone to focus on eating, enjoying the foods and spending time together. Eating as a family helps children learn to identify their need for more or less food and to reduce the need to eat to gain comfort from emotions or other non-hunger motivations.

Benefits

For the child as well as the adults, eating as a family has many benefits. Eating with adults starts to provide some structure to a child's day. They may start to associate a meal with seeing a certain adult or activity. For instance, they may start to recognize that after they eat with Mom or at child care, they will have a nap. Babies will start to recognize that Dad and Mom are both present at a different meal. Your baby, although not ready for all adult foods, will see what you are eating, thus opening the door for accepting new and different foods later on.

As they grow, babies and children learn proper table behaviors, manners and traditions by eating with adults and other family members. Infants and toddlers have opportunities to develop small motor skills as they try to feed themselves. Picking up a pea and bringing it to the mouth is an accomplishment for an infant. Learning that it is very hard to pick up yogurt with hands is also a valuable lesson. Babies also pick up language skills through listening and observing nonverbal interaction at the table.

There has been much research documenting the nutritional as well as social, emotional and psychological growth of children from positive family meal times. When children eat with families they consume a more nutrient-rich diet. They eat more portions of fruits and vegetables and consume higher levels of calcium, protein, iron, fiber and vitamins A, C, E, B-6, and folate.

Although your child is young now, creating the tradition of family meals pays off as your children get older. Children who are exposed to family meals are also more likely to choose healthier foods away from home. Children who eat with their families also consume fewer calories from soft drinks and snack foods. Higher academic performance has also been correlated with family meals. One study found that family discussions increased children's vocabulary even more than reading to them. Better vocabularies help children to do well in all studies. Children also learn how to format their ideas and defend them through family discussions. These skills lead to better students and adults. A study by an anti-substance abuse group, the National Center of Addiction and /Substance Abuse (CASA), found the same results coupled with a decrease in undesirable behaviors. The CASA study showed teens who eat with their families are less likely to smoke cigarettes, consume alcohol or use illegal drugs. Families who eat together tend to have better overall relationships.

To encourage your child to come to the family table, there is one thing you should not do at family meals—bring up unpleasant personal topics not directly related to table manners. If family meal time is the time when the children are reprimanded for previous bad behavior, asked to discuss poor school grades or explain being caught in some infraction, they won't want to attend no matter what you are offering to eat. Keep meal time conversation interesting but not focused on personal problems. Appropriate topics can include discussions about the food, what each family member did or saw that day, plans for a family vacation, neighborhood or even world events. (As your children become older the discussions may become more serious or thought-provoking.) Just don't ask your child why they grabbed the toy from their friend. This should be discussed, but not at dinner.

Avoiding personally unpleasant topics makes the dinner table a safe place for the children, but the adults at the table should still be setting limits on appropriate table manners and behavior. One of the reasons a family should eat together is to learn table manners. Keep in mind that appropriate table manners for a one year-old are different than a ten or fifteen year-old. A three year-old will drop a bit of food. Hopefully your sixteen year-old has this under control. You decide what is appropriate and follow through.

Understanding Satiety

As a parent you will role model positive attitudes toward foods. Hopefully children will be taught to eat to satiety, or until they are full. Children who are served regularly-timed meals will know that they do not have to overeat to sustain themselves until the next time food is offered. They learn to be in touch with their bodies to know when they have had enough, and stop eating. Parents can promote this by letting a child judge when they have had enough food and not forcing them to eat more.

Starting the pattern of eating with your child instills the correct boundaries for when they are older. It also sets the pattern for a growing family. It may be easy to feed one child and then feed yourself or another adult. However, if your family grows, meals will take up too much of your time if you are feeding or cooking for everyone separately. Eating meals together will simplify your life.

Scheduling Family Meals

It is easier to find a time for family meals when your children are young than when they are older. Babies and preschool children don't usually have classes or enrichment programs during the dinner hour. However, as young as school-age, there are opportunities for a child to be away in the early evening. Children are asked to participate in sports, theater presentations, choral groups, music or language lessons, art, dance, or chess to name a few. If you have more than one child scheduling can be difficult. Getting more than one child to and from activities and finding the time to get a meal on the table may seem daunting. You and your partner's evening schedules may also be busy. With all of this going on, if you are not enjoying family meals you will certainly have plenty of excuses not to have them.

There are usually three major reasons why family meals don't happen. The first is scheduling. I cannot solve this one for you. I can only educate you as to the benefits of family meals, and believe that the results of family meals are well worth your efforts to adjust work schedules. The second detriment to family dinners is having the time and energy to get food into the house and on the table. I will address these hurdles in the following sections "Quick and Easy Family Meals" and "Meal Planning". The third detriment to family meals is multifaceted. Many parents avoid family meal time in order to avoid figuring out what to cook to keep everyone happy (hint: nearly impossible) and the unpleasantness of trying to get children to eat, and the accompanying bribing, punishment and other food negotiations and power struggles.

All of this takes place at the time of day when everyone is most tired and hungry, and just wants to relax. Learn to avoid this and you will likely be more willing to figure out the scheduling. Picture you and your family having a pleasant dinner, with interesting conversation and good food. If this is your goal, read on.

Quick and Easy Family Meals

When I shared my ideas for quick meals with my sister, a mother of four, she said "A quick meal is Cheerios and milk." She was right, but for those of you who would like a little variety there are many dinners you can cook and serve within 30 minutes and some in less time than that.

Keep it Simple

Keep in mind that it is better to have a family meal of simple food than to not have a family meal at all because you don't have the time, energy or resources to pull it together. Keeping it simple can be a healthy way to eat. When you do have the time or inclination to cook, make a lot. Plain cooked pasta can be frozen and quickly heated in the microwave or with hot water. Quick dinners can also consist of previously frozen casseroles or soups. Add salad or fruit and you have a meal. Frozen, boxed, canned and convenience foods are allowed. It is better to eat frozen and canned fruits and vegetables than none at all. The microwave, toaster oven and crock pot are all available to help you speed things along. Meals do not need to be 3-6 courses; an entrée and a fruit or vegetable is a job well done. If you have the time and desire to cook, go for it. If not, read on.

The first way to pull off a quick meal is with previous planning. You need to have ingredients in your house and it helps if you know in advance what you are going to make (see "Grocery Shop One Time a Week"). This way you don't have to waste time staring into your refrigerator, freezer or pantry hoping to be inspired. Planning the actual meal need not be difficult. You don't need a cookbook, but for those who prefer a recipe, check out cookbooks that have titles with phrases like: 5 ingredients or less, quick meals, meals in minutes, etc. However, much can be made without a recipe, just follow the ideas below for many quick tasty meals.

Quick and Healthy Meals		
Start With	**Add**	**Serve With**
• Pasta (*any size or shape*) • Dry - cooking time: 10 minutes • Fresh - cooking time: 3 minutes	• Sauce from jar or can or • Drizzle with olive oil and herbs (*garlic, parsley, basil, thyme, oregano*), parmesan cheese or • Frozen vegetables (microwave for approx. 2 min. or drop in with pasta last 3 minutes)	• Premixed salad greens or • fruit
• Corn tortillas (*warm in oven or microwave*) • Flour tortillas (*cold or warm*) • Pita bread	<u>Any of the following:</u> • Canned sliced olives • Corn-from frozen (*serve hot*) • Premixed greens • Scallions, chopped • Grated cheese • Canned refried beans (*hot or cold*) • Low fat meats or fish (*turkey, chicken, shrimp, ground beef*) • Salsa • Sour cream	• Chips or • Fruit or • Rice (*instant rice or basmati cooks in 20 minutes*)
• Rice-basmati (*cooks in 20 minutes*) • Couscous (*cooks in 15 minutes*) • Pasta • Quinoa (*cooks in 15 minutes*)	• Stir-fry vegetables (*fresh or frozen*) • Add: meats (*fresh or cooked poultry, seafood, beef, tofu, or beans*) • Add: garlic powder, soy sauce, ginger powder or use bottled sauce (*Indian, Thai, Chinese*)	• Canned pineapple or • Yogurt or • Fruit Smoothie (*make in blender*)

• Premixed greens	<u>Add any or all:</u> • Beans - canned meats, poultry, seafood (*cooked, leftover*) • Cheese • Corn or peas (*defrosted frozen, fresh or canned*) • Dried fruit: cranberries, raisins • Nuts, seeds • Canned mandarin oranges • Thin slices of apples • Fresh vegetables • Sun dried tomatoes • Artichoke hearts	• Bread • Soup: canned ok • Chips and salsa • Baked potato • Large pretzels with mustard • Chips with melted cheese Salsa
• Prepared pizza crust or • Bagel slices or • Crusty bread sliced length-wise or • Pita bread or • English muffin or • Flour tortilla	• Spaghetti sauce • Cheese • Vegetables (*from frozen or canned*) • Beans (*canned*) • Meats, poultry, seafood • Pesto cheese • Sliced cooked meats (*deli or other*)	• Premixed greens or • Fruit or fruit salad
• Baked potato (*microwave 3-4 minutes*) or wash, poke with fork and cook with time bake	• Cheese • Vegetable (*from frozen*) • Meats, poultry, seafood • Beans • Sour cream • Canned chili	• Premixed salad greens or • Soup (canned or dry) or • Fruit
• Pizza crust or • Bagels-slice or • Crusty bread-slice length-wise or • Pita bread or • English muffin or • Flour tortilla	• Unsweetened applesauce (*cover with cheese then add raisins*) • Sunflower seeds • Refried beans (*cover with garlic, cumin, chili, salsa, top with cheese, then add peppers*) • Corn (*from frozen or canned*)	• Fruit • Premixed greens or • Steamed vegetable(frozen, fresh or canned): broccoli, carrots, peas, spinach or mix

• Any frozen convenience food: pizza, eggrolls, lasagna, burritos, chicken, fish sticks, etc.	• Rice-try brown: basmati or jasmine	• Steamed vegetable (frozen, fresh or canned): broccoli, carrots, peas, spinach, green beans or mix or • Premixed greens

• Canned or frozen soup	• Bread or • Cold sandwich fixings or • Chips or • Baked potato	• Fruit and cheese

• Scrambled eggs	• Soup (*canned*) or • Steamed vegetables (*frozen, fresh or canned*): broccoli, carrots, peas, cauliflower, spinach, green beans or mix	• Bread or • Chips or • Warm tortillas or • Pasta salad

• Tortillas (*for wraps*)	• Sauté onion, pepper • Add: ground beef or tofu • Add tomato sauce, garlic powder, salt, pepper	• Corn on the cob

• Tortillas (*for wrap*) • Try whole wheat	• Tuna, canned salmon, or • Canned chicken, mix with mayonnaise for salad • Humus	• Olives, pickles or fresh cut vegetables or • Tomato soup (canned ok)

• Submarine sandwich Bread	• Deli meats or • Leftover meat, sliced thin or • Tofu • Add: lettuce, onions, pickles	• Fruit or fruit salad • Coleslaw • Bean salad

Most of the quick meals listed include ingredients that can be assembled or left separately for children to try. Whenever possible, let those eating assemble their own finished product from your offerings. This saves you time and allows everyone to customize their meal. Serve baked potatoes, grated cheese, steamed broccoli and canned chili. Let everyone stuff their potato or eat the ingredients separately. Sandwiches can be made quickly, especially when you put the fixings on the table and let everyone assemble what they want to eat. You can also set up a mini salad bar and heat up a can of soup. Be sure to include croutons and see where they end up: in the soup, in the salad or as the main dish for children.

Convenience Foods

There is no shame in using frozen or store-prepared convenience foods. The only caution is the amount of fat and salt in some of these foods. Read the nutrition label or ask your grocer for a nutritional analysis of their prepared foods. If they can't supply you with one ask about the main ingredients and use your best judgment. Anything prepared with cheese will be high in fat as will any fried foods. Foods dressed in a white sauce are most likely high in fat as well. It is hard to see salt, but many prepared Asian dishes, especially those with soy sauce, can be high in sodium.

Optional Pizazz

Your old quick standbys - perhaps hamburgers, baked chicken, grilled meats or macaroni and cheese -can be revitalized with very little effort. To make meals a little more interesting you might consider buying some simmer sauces for the chicken, or adding a portabella mushroom (grilled right along side the meat) to burgers. Grilled meats can be enhanced by letting them marinate (in the refrigerator) during the day. Grilled cheese can be made new by making the adult sandwiches with a more flavorful cheese like Swiss or Gruyere. Interesting spreads can make sandwiches seem new. Try pesto, humus or bruchetta, or ingredients like roasted red peppers, kalamata olives or artichoke hearts.

To keep cooking easy but not boring think about buying different types of familiar foods. Instead of buying the same loaf of white bread, try rye, whole wheat or sourdough bread. Try different shapes of bread, some with hard crusts and some with soft. Tortillas come in different sizes and vary from corn to wheat. Some are green from spinach and others red from peppers. They may taste the same but they will add a lot to the appeal of your foods. Pasta also comes in many different shapes and sizes. Most stores also offer brands of whole wheat or white pasta. Pasta made from potato flour called gnocchi is showing up at many stores (in the dry pasta section), as are frozen or dried tortellini filled with cheeses, meats, spinach, sun dried tomatoes, pesto or even sweet potatoes. Check out your refrigerated and frozen food sections. There is also an abundance of sauces created to give a regional flavor to foods. These are great on grains, as marinades for meat or over noodles. To keep meals healthy check the ingredient labels for fat and sodium content. Over one third of the calories from fat is too much unless it is used sparingly. A sodium content over 20% of the Daily Value (%DV) is also a little on the high side. White rice is just one of many kinds of rice. Rice can be long grain or short grain, brown or white (the brown is healthier) or it can be a totally different type such as Jasmine, Basmati, or wild rice. Each kind of rice has its own flavor. Beware of flavored rice in a box; the flavor is usually just salt with a few herbs or spices added.

Every time you create a new quick meal, write down the ingredients or name of the dish on a list. Collect ideas from cookbooks or friends. Over time this list will provide you with more than enough ideas to feed your family in a hurry.

Meal Planning

For some of us cooking a meal is not the problem, it's just that with daily commotion, we don't have a meal in mind. Once we decide what to eat, it usually means a trip to the store, adding to the commotion. It seems to be an endless circle. Take heart. With a little planning meal preparation time can become an easy - and maybe even an enjoyable - task.

Plan for the Week

To get started, set aside one time each week that you can actually think without interruptions. You only need about 15 minutes. Make a chart with columns for each day of the week and rows for "What's Happening," "Who Is Eating" and "What To Serve." Then fill in the first rows as accurately as possible. Under "What's Happening": if your kids have a class right before or during dinner, write this down. If you are always at a meeting on Monday nights, write this down. For "Who Is Eating": write in the number of people or their names if dietary needs are an issue. Keep in mind invited guests too. Now you are ready to decide what you might serve.

When choosing "What to Serve," consider all the information on your chart. The "What's Happening" row will help you know how much time you will have to prepare a meal. On evenings when you get home half an hour before dinner you will choose something easy like pasta, grilled meat or fish or frozen entrees (store bought or previously cooked and frozen by you). If you use a crock pot, you need to remind yourself to start the dinner that morning. On evenings when you are home an hour or more before dinner you may choose to cook something that takes longer to prepare or cook, like a casserole, soup, stew or a favorite but more complex recipe. "Who is Eating" also comes into play. If it is just you and the kids you may want to keep it simple: grilled cheese and canned soup. If you have guests you may want to have several side dishes along with the entrée. If you are gone and your spouse is cooking, check in with them. What does he want to make? One last tip: for freshness, include leafy greens, fish and meats earlier in the week and heartier or frozen foods later in the week.

Dinner Ideas

For some, actually deciding what to serve is the hardest task. There are several methods that can help you in this process. First, make a list of every dinner that you can make, including dinners from canned and frozen foods and hot or cold meals. You may find that this gives you enough choice. If not, walk through the frozen food section or thumb through a cookbook. Sometimes thinking about different food categories helps. List all of the beef, pork, lamb, chicken or fish dishes. Then list all of those from eggs, cheese, beans and pasta. Don't forget about stir fries, wraps, or breakfast for dinner (pancakes, waffles, French toast or omelets). As you try new meal recipes or ideas, keep a list of them. For help in developing menus, list each dinner or recipe name on this chart. You'll be surprised how full it eventually becomes.

	No Cook	Boil or Steam	Bake or Microwave	Grill	Stir Fry or Pan Fry	Broil	Stew or Slow Cook
Poultry							
Beef							
Pork/Lamb							
Bean/Tofu							
Fish							
Egg							
Cheese							
Noodles/Rice							

There are other strategies for creating a selection of meals. Some people don't mind eating the same thing all week. If this works for you, make a large casserole or cook a turkey or chicken and eat it all week. Others may choose to make variations of the same food. A turkey can be eaten roasted the first night, as part of a stir fry the next night, in wraps or sandwiches the next and as soup the following night. For those who prefer different foods each night, choose foods from different food categories each night. You may choose a beef dish for the first meal, chicken for the second meal, fish for the third meal, etc. If you really like variety and foods from different cultures, you could set up your meal choices by nationality, eating Italian on Sunday, Chinese on Monday, etc.

Sample Weekly Plan

	Sunday	Monday	Tuesday	Wednesday	Thursday	Friday	Saturday
What's Happening	Soccer game, home 6:00	Mom leaves for yoga at 6:00	Business meeting-Randy	Soccer practice, home 5:30	Home	Soccer practice, home 5:00	Home
Who's Eating	All family	Kids and Dad	Mom and Kids	All family	All family and Johnsons	All family	All Family
What to Serve	Take out pizza	Burgers, buns, coleslaw, corn	Stir Fry w/chicken, rice	Canned chili, chips, canned pineapple	Fish, baked potatoes, broccoli, salad, brownies	Chinese noodle soup with chicken and peas, eggrolls	Steak, mixed vegetables, sweet potato fries

If you don't want to create new menus every week use the Rotation Menu plan. This is usually used in residential institutions or schools but it can be successful at home. Start by setting up one week of menus. If you want, you can reuse this menu over and over; however, meal time may get a little boring. But if you can expand this menu to include three weeks, it will probably have enough variety to let you use this plan continuously. If the three week plan works, your may find that you need a fall/winter and spring/summer plan to accommodate heavier and lighter foods. Keep in mind that three weeks of menus does not need to include twenty-one different meals. For example, if you family enjoys pasta, you can include it as often as you'd like. If you eat out every Wednesday, include that in the plan. It's fine to pick up take out or go to fast food, but plan for it-don't go there by default. This becomes habit forming, expensive and usually unhealthy.

Simple Three Week Rotating Menu

Week	Sunday	Monday	Tuesday	Wednesday	Thursday	Friday	Saturday
1	Chili Chips Salsa Salad	Vegetable Stir fry with chicken Brown rice Miso broth	Lentil soup Bread Salad	Pasta and sauce Meatballs Fruit salad	Roast beef Baked potato Steamed vegetable	Pizza Salad Apple sauce	Grilled fish Corn (on cob, canned or frozen) Spinach salad
2	Bean and cheese burritos Salad	Lasagna Steamed carrots or peas	Hamburgers and buns French fries Fruit salad or coleslaw	Tuna (or salmon) melt on English muffin Steamed vegetable	Baked chicken Mashed potatoes salad	Dinner out	Steak Rice or cous-cous Vegetable stir fry
3	Fish taco with cabbage Fruit salad	Lamb chops Steamed vegetable bread	Pasta and sun dried tomatoes, pine nuts Cheese- sticks Salad	Beef stew Cornbread	Black bean soup Nachos Green salad	Pizza Salad	Quiche or omelets Potato Steamed broccoli

102

Make a Shopping List

Now that you know what you are going to eat for the week, make a shopping list. Also include staples and breakfast, lunch and snack foods. Some people keep an ongoing list for all family members to add to when something runs out. (You have to train them to do this.) Others have purchased or personally pre-made lists with items already listed. Then you just need to check off what to buy and add a few other items. Take the list and go shopping. If all is well you can buy everything at once for the week. Whatever you need for each evening's meal will be in your house.

Plan for the Unexpected

However, plan for mistakes and miscalculations. Have a few items in the freezer or pantry that can be brought out in case you forgot to buy something, there is no time to cook what you thought you were going to make, or more or less people than expected need to be fed. Frozen pizzas, bread, lasagna and meatballs, canned soups, beans and sauces, and dry pasta can all help to make quick meals. Other helpful items include tortillas (they can be frozen), frozen vegetables, eggs, cheese and boxes of soup broth. By keeping some basic ingredients on hand, you can prepare quick, nutritious meals at a moment's notice.

Dry Goods

✓ Cold breakfast cereals without added fat or sugars

✓ Hot breakfast cereals- quick cook oats

✓ Pasta, including fettuccine, spirals, lasagna

✓ Quick cooking brown rice

✓ Couscous

✓ Quinoa

✓ Polenta

✓ Popcorn

✓ Raisins

✓ Dried fruit

- ✓ Instant soups: soup cups, noodle soups
- ✓ Dried black or pinto bean flakes
- ✓ Aseptically packaged tofu (keeps unrefrigerated for 6 months to 1 year)
- ✓ Low salt vegetable broth: powder, cubes, boxed or canned
- ✓ Boxed macaroni and cheese
- ✓ Pilaf

Canned Foods (canned goods should be used within one year)

- ✓ Baked beans
- ✓ Canned beans, including kidney, garbanzo, black, pinto, etc.
- ✓ Canned tomatoes, tomato sauce, tomato paste
- ✓ Canned pumpkin, peaches, pears, pineapple
- ✓ Unsweetened applesauce
- ✓ Low fat, low salt soups
- ✓ Chili beans
- ✓ Fat-free refried beans
- ✓ Spaghetti sauce
- ✓ Salsa
- ✓ Sauces: soy, thai, oyster, sweet and sour
- ✓ Vegetable oil spray

Perishable Foods

- ✓ Pre-washed salad mix or spinach
- ✓ Cut up fruit, vegetables
- ✓ Soft fruit, peaches, plums, berries
- ✓ Milk

Semi-Perishable Foods

- ✓ Onions
- ✓ Garlic
- ✓ Potatoes
- ✓ Yams or sweet potatoes
- ✓ Winter squash
- ✓ Green cabbage
- ✓ Carrots
- ✓ Celery
- ✓ Apples
- ✓ Oranges
- ✓ Bananas
- ✓ Whole grain bread (may be frozen)
- ✓ Whole wheat tortillas (may be frozen)
- ✓ Corn tortillas (may be frozen)
- ✓ Miso (will last up to a year when refrigerated)
- ✓ Cheese: brick, slices, grated
- ✓ Eggs
- ✓ Tofu, tempeh
- ✓ Deli slices
- ✓ Fresh pasta or noodles

Frozen Foods (should be used within 6 months)

- ✓ Juice concentrate
- ✓ Frozen mixed vegetables
- ✓ Frozen corn, peas, broccoli, spinach, carrots

- ✓ Frozen bananas
- ✓ Frozen berries
- ✓ Frozen chopped onions
- ✓ Frozen diced bell peppers
- ✓ Ground meat patties
- ✓ Vegetarian burgers or frozen meats in individual servings
- ✓ Frozen dinners: casseroles, pizza, appetizers
- ✓ Breads: sliced, tortillas, naan, pizza crusts, pita, bagels, hot dog and hamburger buns
- ✓ Desserts
- ✓ Prepared meats, chicken, seafood

Seasonings and Condiments

- ✓ Herbs and spices: cinnamon, ginger, cloves, ground cumin, cayenne, chili powder, red pepper flakes, curry powder, basil, oregano, black pepper, salt
- ✓ Soy sauce
- ✓ Seasoned rice vinegar
- ✓ Balsamic vinegar
- ✓ Cider vinegar
- ✓ Mustard
- ✓ Ketchup
- ✓ Mayonnaise
- ✓ Jam, jelly
- ✓ Molasses
- ✓ Maple syrup
- ✓ Sugar, honey
- ✓ Olive oil

This plan may sound like it takes more effort than the time you will save. But once you get into the routine of keeping a shopping list and choosing dinners in advance you will save time, especially if you can limit grocery shopping to once a week.

Grocery Shop One Time a Week

One time a week, is that possible? Yes. It's not only possible, it's practical. Shopping one time a week saves time. It may take a couple hours to shop once a week, but that is less time than it will take if you shop two to three times, even if you are just "running in for a few things." It's almost impossible to get to the store, shop and get home in less than 45 minutes, especially if you have children in tow. Just before dinner is one of the busiest times to shop and therefore the store is crowded and lines are long. Shopping once a week should result in more time to do other things. Also, if you make it a point to do the once-a-week shopping before or after peak shopping times, lines will be shorter.

Shopping once a week will save money. The less times you go into the store, the less opportunity to buy impulse items, especially if you are shopping from a list. There is also less opportunity for your children to beg for food items you rather they not have, especially before dinner. The less often you go to the store, the less gas you will use. (Extra bonus: fewer trips results in less greenhouse gases!) Grocery foods cost less than restaurant foods. Having a plan for dinner and sticking with it allows you to avoid the cost of desperate take-out or restaurant meals.

Having the food you need in the house results in a healthier diet for the whole family. Restaurant food is almost always higher in fat and salt than food prepared at home. Restaurants also tend to serve larger portions. At home, you can fill your plate with vegetables and keep the carbohydrates and proteins under control, and there are usually no appetizers or desserts to tempt you.

Shopping once a week can lower your stress level, by eliminating one daily job.. How many times have you experienced that awful feeling when asking yourself, "What am I going to make for dinner?" How many times have you wandered through the grocery store at 5:00 pm trying to decide what to make for dinner, thinking, *Did we have chicken this week? Do I have any potatoes at home? I wonder if they still sell those frozen meatballs?* This can be an especially unenjoyable trip if you are running late or the children are begging for junk foods.

Shopping once a week can be done. I have been doing it for ten years - with kids in tow. If you need to buy some things later in the week, like fresh meats, seafood and milk, see if you can get another household member to pick them up for you. Some neighborhoods are serviced by milk and produce delivery. If you do need to go two times a week, schedule it. By using a weekly plan and shopping once a week with a list, all the decision making and shopping is done. The food is at home waiting for you. Just walk in the door, check your plan, and cook. It's not exactly as great as a massage or a quiet hour with a book, but it is one less worry and one less errand.

Play it Safe

Keep it Clean

Most of us keep our kitchens clean, but harmful germs and bacteria cannot be seen, smelled or tasted. In order to help keep ourselves and families healthy it is necessary to know how to prevent the growth and distribution of harmful organisms. First, as most of you know, wash your hands with warm soapy water before and after food preparation. Antibacterial soap is not necessary, but washing for at least 30 seconds lets the soap dislodge germs and running water will wash them away. Children's toys, dishes and cutting boards can also be sufficiently cleaned with warm soapy water. If running water or soap is not available, any hand gel containing a 62% solution of propyl alcohol will clean you hands. These gels come in small containers great for keeping in a car, purse or backpack.

There was great controversy over which cutting board is more sanitary: plastic or wood. Testing has shown that both are a good choice but require cleaning after each use with warm soapy water. Some plastic cutting boards have the advantage of being dishwasher-safe. If not washed properly, cutting boards and knives can lead to cross-contamination (occurring when residue from a food being prepared with a knife or on a board is transmitted to another food). For example, if you are making raw hamburger patties on a cutting board, it needs to be washed thoroughly before you use the same board to slice tomatoes. If the board is not washed, bacteria cooked away in the hamburger but left on the cutting board can transfer to the tomato, which is eaten raw. Ideally you would have separate cutting boards, one for raw meat and one for cooked meats, and another for foods such as bread, fresh fruits and vegetables.

Sponges can also cause cross-contamination. After wiping up meat juices, if a sponge is merely rinsed it could transfer bacteria to the next surface. Sponges are a great place for germs to grow. Germs grow well in warm (room temperature) and moist places. If you use sponges, wash or replace them daily. There are several ways to keep sponges clean. One way is to let them soak in a bleach and water solution when not in use. This solution should be ¼ teaspoon bleach to 1 quart of water, made fresh each day. Unfortunately the bleach can cause the sponges to fall apart quickly. Another way to clean them is to throw them in with your clothes wash or wash them on the top shelf of the dishwasher. Two minutes in the microwave will also kill germs and bacteria in a wet sponge (dry sponges could catch on fire).

The top shelf of the dishwasher is fine for cleaning sippy cups, but it might not clean the inside of the lid due to all the plastic folds and internal spaces. If your child's cup uses a straw, a dishwasher cannot clean in the straw. Rinse it in warm soapy water and let it air dry for best results.

If you want your kitchen even cleaner, you can sanitize it inexpensively with a bleach solution of ¼ teaspoon of bleach to 1 quart of water, mixed daily. After cleaning your kitchen surfaces and knife blades, simply spray them with this solution. It is strong enough to kill germs but will not harm anyone or any surface. Don't wipe it off; it will evaporate in a few minutes. There are also sanitizing wipes that produce the same results; they cost more but are convenient. However, eating surfaces sanitized with many of these wipes require a water rinse.

Food Storage

How long can foods be frozen and refrigerated? Breast milk can be frozen up to six months in a deep freeze, six days in the refrigerator and 6 hours at room temperature. Raw meats need to be refrigerated or in the freezer within 30 minutes of leaving the store. Use a cooler packed with ice if this is not possible. When storing food in the freezer, mark it with a date, including the year. It's amazing how fast time goes by.

Food	In Refrigerator	In Freezer
Eggs, fresh, in shells	3 weeks	Don't freeze
Raw yolks, whites	2-4 days	1 year
Hard cooked eggs	1 week	Don't freeze
Liquid pasteurized eggs or egg substitutes, opened, unopened	10 days	1 year
Mayonnaise, refrigerate after opening	2 months	3-5 months
Frozen prepared foods	Keep in freezer	2-3 months
Soups and stews	3-4 days	2-3 months
Store prepared or homemade egg, chicken, tuna, ham and macaroni salads	3-5 days	Don't freeze
Fresh beef	3-5 days	6-12 months
Fresh pork	3-5 days	4-6 months
Fresh veal	3-5 days	4-6 months
Hamburger and stew meat	1-2 days	3-4 months
Ground turkey, veal, pork, lamb or a mixture	1-2 days	3-4 months
Leftover cooked meat and meat dishes	3-4 days	3-4 months
Gravy and meat broth	1-2 days	2-3 months
Fresh chicken or turkey, whole	12 days	1 year
Chicken or turkey pieces	1-2 days	9 months
Leftover cooked poultry dishes	3-4 days	4-6 months
Leftover poutry pieces, plain	3-4 days	6 months
Leftover poultry covered with gravy or broth	1-2 days	1-3 months
Leftover chicken nuggets, patties	1-2 days	1-3 months
Leftover fried chicken	3-4 days	4 months
Hotdogs, lunch meats, opened package	1 week	1-2 months
Hotdogs, lunch meats, upopened package	2 weeks	1-2 months

Keep in mind that germ growth is most active between 40 degrees and 140 degrees Fahrenheit. Most hot food can be left at room temperature for 2 hours maximum. The same applies to food served cold such as luncheon meats, salads, dips and sliced fruits and vegetables. If food is left out for over 2 hours, (it's easy to become distracted with children), it is best to throw the food out. Cow's milk will only be safe up to 2 hours out of refrigeration. Only serve what you estimate your child will consume; you can always get them more. Once a child uses a bottle, cup or bowl, the remaining food or drink should be thrown away, not refrigerated for another use. How often does the same half gallon of milk get put on the table at your house? If you don't use up the milk in the original container after having it out of the refrigerator 2 times, consider pouring needed milk for the meal or snack into a small pitcher. This keeps the rest of the milk refrigerated.

Leftovers need special consideration. Reheating these foods will not kill the potential germs and bacteria if they had 2 hours in which to grow. Foods kept out less than 2 hours can be refrigerated and reheated or served cold within 3 days. Reheating should be done quickly in a hot oven. Leftovers need to be brought to an internal temperature of at least 165 degrees within 15 minutes; liquids should be brought to a boil before they are considered safe to eat. Doggie bag foods from restaurants fall into the 2 hour rule as well. If you go to a movie after the restaurant, don't take food home unless it will be in a car that is less than 40 degrees.

Even though your mother may have done it, foods should never be left to defrost at room temperature. While the inside of the meat is still frozen, the outside is between 40 and 140 degrees Fahrenheit, where germs grow fastest. Defrosting foods is best done gradually, in the refrigerator. Refrigerators should be between 35 and 40 degrees Fahrenheit. Keep raw animal products wrapped so their juices do not drip on to other foods. Meats brought home from the grocery will probably need to be put in plastic bags as the store wrap may leak. Meats take a long time to defrost. A one inch thick steak will take 12-14 hours and a one inch thick package of ground meat may take as long as 24 hours. Roasts and large turkeys can take from 3-7 hours per pound to defrost, depending on their size.

Defrosting takes planning, but life doesn't always happen that way. If you need to use frozen meat immediately, you can microwave it, but only if you will be cooking it immediately. Microwave ovens begin to cook the meat, and any meat between the temperatures of 40 and 140 degrees is a perfect place for bacteria and germs to multiply rapidly. The only way to stop this growth is to cook it immediately at full temperature. Cold running water can be used to defrost smaller frozen items or seafood but does not work fast enough for most frozen meats.

Packed Lunches or Snacks

If you are packing a snack or meal, remember the 2 hour rule. If the snack will be stored outside of refrigeration for longer, there are several solutions. As children need a maximum of only 2 glasses of milk a day, leave the milk at home and bring water. Choose less perishable snacks such as whole fruit, raw vegetables, beans, deli meats, dried foods, cheese and yogurt. Keep snacks cool by first cooling them in the refrigerator and then placing them in coolers or a lined lunch box. Place ice packs in with the foods. Frozen juice boxes or yogurt tubes keep other foods cool as the yogurt and juice thaw.

Cooking

There are different cooking temperatures for various cuts of meat and fish. The only way to tell if meat is properly cooked is to use a food thermometer. The following lists the internal temperature of properly cooked foods.

Food Type	Degree Fahrenheit
Liquid soups, gravies, sauces	212
Poultry, until juices run clear	180
Whole turkey, stuffed	180
Pork, ground poultry and poultry mixes	175
Whole turkey, unstuffed	170
Leftover casseroles and other dishes, stuffing (*in cooked bird*)	165
Ground red meats and pork, egg dishes	160

Roasts and Steaks	Fahrenheit
Medium rare	145
Medium	170
Well done	180

Temperature cannot be judged by touch or sight. Meat thermom-
eters can be purchased at most grocery stores and at kitchen shops.
Before using the thermometer, make sure it is correctly calibrated.
Is it registering the correct temperature? Calibration requires two
tests. First bring a small pot of water to boil. Place the thermometer in the water for 2 minutes. It should read 212 degrees. If the
temperature is higher or lower, use a crescent wrench and turn the
hex nut so the needle is at 212 degrees. Next, totally fill a large
glass with ice and then water. Place the thermometer in the ice and
wait a few minutes. If the needle does not point to 32 degrees, turn
the hex hut until the needle points to 32 degree. Try this test again,
readjust if necessary. Now the thermometer is ready for use.

If using a marinade, throw it away after removing the meat. Do
not pour it over the cooked meat - germs and bacteria from the
raw meat are present in this liquid. Also, do not serve the meat in
the dish that was used for marinating or holding raw meat before
cooking unless it was thoroughly cleaned. Marinating should be
done in the refrigerator, not at room temperature. Again, all raw
meats should be kept between 40 and 140 degrees. The safe way
to cool a large amount of a thick stew, casserole or soup is in small
batches, less than 3 inches thick. Anything thicker will allow the
outside to cool while the inside core is still warm, growing germs
and bacteria.

Chapter 6

CONFESSIONS OF A NUTRITIONIST LIVING WITH CHILDREN

I spend my professional time speaking with parents about how to encourage their children to eat healthy foods. I spend my personal time as a mother of a ten and five -year-old. My ten-year-old daughter tries many new foods and eats a variety of foods and cuisines. She loves channa masala at the Indian restaurants, curry at the Thai and Vietnamese restaurants, almost anything at the Ethiopian restaurant, Chinese noodles, burritos and pizza.

My five year-old is definitely testing my theories about feeding children, as he prefers unhealthy (fun) carbohydrate foods to all else. Top on his list are doughnuts, followed by cookies, candy, anything chocolate, brownie energy bars, dry cereal, and cheese crackers. In the non-carbohydrate categories he will eat pizza, grilled cheese, mac and cheese made only with parmesan, ice cream, yogurt frozen in a popsicle mold, French fries and fried fish. Every now and then when the planets are properly aligned he may eat salmon. He will not try or taste most new foods offered, even if his sister eats them and tells him they are good.

Did I mention that my son does not take or eat lunch at school? In this he is insistent. So for breakfast he eats a healthy dry cereal and (chocolate) milk, no lunch, snack after school, dinner, and snack before bed. I choose what to serve for dinner. Due to my son's narrow preference he usually eats very little at dinner, sometimes just rice or bread and a few cucumbers. He tells me most nights that, "This is a bad dinner, there are no doughnuts." But he does sit with the family every night and talks to us, learning appropriate table manners and social interaction. He is exposed to a wide range of foods as I enjoy cooking and pull from Italian, Thai, Chinese, Indian, Middle Eastern and African recipes.

Now, my son does not have access to many of the above mentioned carbohydrates, but due to parties, holidays, celebrations, grandparents, and play dates these foods appear more often than I would like. At parties I allow my son to eat what he wants. Candy brought home from a party is permitted in what is known in my house as "the candy of the day" (one piece allowed a day). My daughter also eats these candies but likes only the less decadent ones, hard candies and soft fruit flavored chews. She does not like chocolate or even birthday cake. As my kids see their grandparents only two to three times a year, I don't insist that they follow my guidelines. It is their job to spoil my children.

Some nights my son chooses to eat nothing. This is his choice. He is not punished for this choice; hunger will make a better impression on him than any adult rational I may try. So it goes, night after night. I cook; he rarely eats the main course. I do believe that by offering choices I am doing a good job. Does it bother me? Only in that I don't get to have that good feeling when others enjoy the foods we serve. But after seeing certain foods for years, he is starting to ask for tastes of several dishes. The techniques and strategies are working; they are just taking longer than they did for my daughter who will taste almost anything and can find something she wants to eat at almost any restaurant.

Yes, I do bake cookies and muffins with my kids when they ask me to, and yes, I let them pick out store-bought "fun food" to have at home like cookies, crackers and chips. They eat these foods as part of a snack after school and before bed time- one fun food and then healthy foods if they are still hungry.

So where am I going with all of this? I believe that my daughter is doing fine nutritionally and that my son is doing okay. He is probably getting enough of what he needs, but if I rated his diet as a dietician I would give it a "C+" and I would give my daughter an "A-". But I don't think I have anything to gain as a parent by forcing my son to eat certain foods or by forbidding others. My parenting is not a "C+" because his diet is one. My son is only five. He is active, smart, happy, and appears to be just the right weight for himself. He doesn't overeat even when having fun foods. We don't argue about food. We seem to be doing fine, most of the time. How will this turn out? When he is eighteen I will be able to tell the end of this story.

So I offer this book as a professional who has worked as a cook in a child care center for three years, worked with Seattle-area child care centers through the county health department for three years, taught nutrition education to parents with young children through the local community center and who has acted as a private consultant and counselor for twelve years. But I also offer this book as a parent. As a parent I try to do my best, but sometimes my emotions and my desire to just "get through the day" influence my choices more than the parenting book I just read. I do the best I can; I try to see the forest from the trees, and maintain a sense of humor. However, I am sticking to my nutritional beliefs and the specific techniques I know will enable my children to become independent, healthy and emotionally-grounded adults. It works for me and it will work for you and your children.

RESOURCES

Feeding

Meals without Squeals: Child Care Feeding Guide and Cookbook, Berman, Christine, MPH, RD, Fromer, Jacki, Bull Publishing Company, 2006.

Feeding Your Child for Lifelong Health, Susan B. Roberts, Ph.D., Melvin B. Heyman M.D., Lisa Tracy, Bantam Book, 1999

Child of Mine: Feeding with Love and Good Sense, Satter, Ellyn Bull, Publishing Company, 2000.

How to Get Your Kid to Eat....But Not Too Much, Satter, Ellyn Bull, Publishing Company, 1987

Nutrition and Healthy Foods

The World's Healthiest Foods, Essential Guide for the Healthiest Way of Eating, Mateljan, George, George Mateljan Foundation, 2007

What to Eat. Nestle, Marion. North Point Press, 2006

www.CSPI.com, Center For Science in the Public Interest

Allergies and the Environment

How to Manage Your Child's Life-Threatening Allergies: Practical Tips for Everyday Life, Coss, Linda Marienhoff Plumtree Press, 2004

Understanding and Managing Your Child's Food Allergies, Sicherer, Scott H., M.D.. John Hopkins, University Press, 2006

www.foodallergy.org, The Food Allergy Network

www.ewg.org, The Environmental Working Group

www.healthychild.org, Healthy Child, Healthy World

Cookbooks

Quick and Easy Recipes from the New York Times, Bittman, Mark, Broadway Books, 2007

Saving Dinner: The Menus, Recipes and Shopping Lists to Bring your Family Back to the Table, Ely, Leanne, Ballentine Books, 2003

Feeding the Whole Family: Whole Foods Recipes for Babies, Young children and Their Parents, Lair, Cynthia, Moon Smile Press, 1997

The Peaceful Palate, Raymond, Jennifer, Heart and Soul Publications, 1992

Feeding the Kids: The Flexible, No-Battles, Healthy Eating System for the Whole Family, Gould, Pamela, Mancala Publishing, LLC,2007

Parenting

Touchpoints: the Essential Reference, Brazelton, T. Berry, M.D., Addison-Wesley Publishing, 1992

Touchpoints: Three to Six, Brazelton, T. Berry, M.D., Sparrow, Joshua D. M.D., Merloyd Lawrence Books 2001

Becoming the Parent You Want to Be: A Sourcebook of Strategies for the First Five Years, Davis, Laura, Keyser, Janis, Broadway Books, 1997

Mommy! I Need to Go Potty: A Parent's Guide to Toilet Training, Faull, Jan, M.Ed., Raefield-Roberts, Publishers; Parenting Press, 1996.

Darn good advice, Jan Faull, Hauppauge, N.Y.: Barron's, 2006, c2005.

Your Baby and Child: From Birth to Age Five, Leach, Penelope, Alfred A. Knopf, 2002

Positive Discipline, Nelson, Jane, Ed.D., First Ballantine Books Edition 1987, Second Revised Edition, 1996

The Baby Book: Everything You Need to Know About Your Baby-From Birth to Age Two, Sears, William, M.D., Sears, Martha, R.N., Little, Brown and co., 1993

The Discipline Book: How to Have a better-Behaved Child From Birth to Age Ten, Sears, William, M.D., Sears, Martha, R.N., Little, Brown and co., 1995

www.Kellymoms.com

Acknowledgements

I would like to thank those who supported me during the writing of this book. To my husband Chris, who pushed me when I needed it, encouraged me to follow my instincts, and provided an endless supply of much needed technical support. Next, the parents, grandparents and nannies who have attended my classes at Bellevue Community College. Your concerns, comments, observations and questions have helped me to grow in so many ways. I am honored that you chose to share your lives and the lives of your babies with me. It was such a gift to watch your babies start to discover themselves and their world during our time together. Finally to my colleagues and friends: Maria College, Gwen Glew, Jill Beilinson, Jodi Negrin, Kimberly Mathai, Laura Freeman, who provided information, opinions and support when ever I asked.

Index

Made in the USA
Lexington, KY
13 January 2012